VEGAN  *in an*
INSTANT

103 PLANT-BASED RECIPES FOR YOUR INSTANT POT®

VEGAN in an INSTANT

103 PLANT-BASED RECIPES FOR YOUR INSTANT POT®

Use of the trademark is authorized by Instant Brands Inc., owner of Instant Pot®

MARINA DELIO

ALPHA

CONTENTS

SNACKS & APPETIZERS

ABOUT THE AUTHOR

Marina Delio of YummyMummyKitchen.com is a recipe developer and lifestyle influencer with a passion for cooking plant-based and nourishing meals for her family. Her recipes have been featured in *Cooking Light, Southern Living, Mother Earth Living, Santa Barbara Magazine,* on Saveur.com, Prevention.com, Self.com, FitnessMagazine.com, CountryLiving.com, Health.com, Glamour.com, and on the *Martha Stewart Show.* Marina's mission is to share the beauty of whole foods with others, helping them live happier, healthier lives. She shares how-to videos of her latest plant-based creations on her website and on social media, which have garnered millions of views. When she's not cooking, photographing, or writing about food, you can find Marina driving the carpool, walking her two dogs, recharging with a run or yoga class, or shopping at the Santa Barbara Farmers Market.

ACKNOWLEDGMENTS

I would like to thank the DK Publishing team for reaching out to me to work on this cookbook. It's a privilege to get to help others eat well, and I'm so grateful for the opportunity. I'd especially like to thank my editor, Alexandra Elliott, for making the process smooth, organized, and fun. Thanks to Dana Angelo White for testing every single recipe in this book, giving helpful feedback, and compiling nutritional information.

To my literary agent, Coleen O'Shea, for always being there to help guide me through the publishing world.

To my mom for taking my recipe-testing leftovers, fully embracing plant-based eating, and supporting my endeavors always. And to my dad who helped shaped the foodie I am today.

To my husband, Phil, whose support has allowed me to build my career from home with our girls over the past 10 years, and for his enthusiasm for plant-based foods.

To my kids, for their encouragement and sense of humor when cooking experiments don't go quite as planned. We will forever laugh about eating the same lentil dish five nights in a row until I got the recipe just right.

INTRODUCTION

When I first started my food blog nearly 10 years ago, I had no intention of moving in a primarily plant-based direction. Though I had vegan friends, I thought surely they were starving, protein deficient, and no longer enjoying the delicious foods I was passionate about. Years later, I began to do my own research, reading the science from plant-based doctors such as Dr. Michael Greger, and following strong, thriving, plant-based athletes. I learned that it's possible to eat a satisfying plant-based diet while maintaining balanced nutrition. Not only that, but I learned that vegan dishes could still contain all the umami, creaminess, textures, and flavor that omnivores enjoy. As a lifelong animal lover, it's a diet with which I'm a lot more comfortable! I'm thrilled now to be helping others fall in love with nourishing, whole plant foods that are a bit gentler on most bodies, animals, and the earth.

The addition of the Instant Pot to my kitchen has been a game changer as a busy mom and plant-based home chef. Rice, whole grains, and legumes that traditionally take hours to soak and cook are now a breeze. I love that I no longer use cans of beans or plastic-wrapped, pre-cooked rice. The Instant Pot has made plant-based cooking healthier, easier, quicker, cheaper, and more eco-friendly.

This book will help you whip up delicious and easy one-pot meals—such as curry, chili, minestrone, and risotto—so you can spend more time with your family. You'll also find special occasion treats like chocolate cake topped with ganache and berries. Enjoy!

–Marina Delio

Marina Delio

YummyMummyKitchen.com

REFERENCES

There is a wealth of information online for plant-based pressure cooking. Two of my favorite resources are the Instant Pot website's cooking time tables (http://www.instantpot.com/instantpot-cooking-time/), and the vegan Instant Pot groups on Facebook.

PLANT-BASED FAST AND EASY

Your Instant Pot electric countertop appliance is ideal for plant-based cooking. It pressure cooks, slow cooks, steams, sautés, and makes yogurt—all in one pot! The Instant Pot makes it quick and easy to prepare whole, nutritious foods.

WHOLE FOODS FOR BUSY PEOPLE

The Instant Pot helps busy people enjoy the nourishing food they want without spending hours in the kitchen. As a busy mom, I love that I can "set and forget" our dinner to cook in the Instant Pot. I can help my kids with their homework without fussing over a pot on the stove or in the oven. Perfectly creamy risotto without stirring? No problem!

QUICK AND EFFICIENT

Cooking under pressure enables you to prepare whole foods in half the time. With the Instant Pot, you can finally make perfectly tender beans without any soaking. Cooking brown rice and black beans all at once is easy using the pot-in-pot method (cooking both foods simultaneously by placing an additional pot inside the Instant Pot). Firmer vegetables, such as beets, traditionally take 40 minutes or more to roast but are sweet and tender after just 20 minutes under pressure.

ONE-POT MEALS

The Instant Pot takes up very little space on your counter, and cleanup is a breeze because you're only using one pot. These self-contained meals are ideal for people who care about eating well but need doing so to be easy. With it's many functions, you can sauté and pressure cook all in the same pot, developing the best possible flavor. The **Warm** function will keep your meal ready until you are!

SAFE AND USER-FRIENDLY

My first Instant Pot sat in its box, unopened, for months. I was intimidated and concerned about safety. After preparing my first dish, though, I was hooked. The Instant Pot is actually incredibly simple to use, and it's safe. It's equipped with safety mechanisms that the old-fashioned pressure cookers about which we hear horror stories simply didn't have. When used correctly, there is very little risk. You'll have great success following the step-by-step instructions for each of the recipes in the book.

Choosing Your Model

There are many models of Instant Pot with varying sizes and features. The language on the panels changes, but they all essentially work the same. They come in 3-, 6-, and 8-quart sizes. The recipes in this book were developed in a 6-quart pot, which is a good size for an average family. Explore the functions on the different pots before making your purchase.

Depending on which model you own, you may notice subtle differences in the organization of the controls, as well as the names of some of the programs. Some older models may have a **Manual** program button, which is the equivalent of the **Pressure Cook** button on most newer models. Some older models may also have a **Start** button, while the programs on newer models may start automatically, beginning 10 seconds after program selection.

Dietary Tags

Whatever your dietary needs, you can make the Instant Pot work for you. Each recipe is marked with an icon to indicate whether it's free of common allergens.

g_f Gluten-free

s_f Soy-free

o_f Oil-free

n_f Nut-free

GET TO KNOW YOUR INSTANT POT

Before jumping into cooking with the Instant Pot, it's important to understand how this amazing appliance works. Familiarize yourself with these basic concepts to make your pressure cooking safe and successful.

COOKING UNDER PRESSURE

When you cook under pressure, your pot becomes airtight and pressurizes inside, increasing temperature and forcing steam into your food to cook it much quicker than with traditional methods. When using any pressure function, four factors affect outcome.

(1) SEALING: Without proper sealing to prevent air from escaping the pot, your pot will not come to pressure. Proper sealing is critical to achieving the expected results in the Instant Pot. Once your pot is sealed with the lid firmly in place, it will slowly begin to build pressure inside.

The lid will only lock into place if the silicone sealing ring is properly placed inside the lid. If the lid isn't properly in place, an error message will display on the LCD display. If you remove the lid to add an ingredient and then attempt to close and lock the lid back in place when there's still hot food in the inner pot, the pressure may still be too high and the pot may not seal. If this occurs, simply wait a few minutes for the contents to cool down a bit, and then replace the lid. Once the lid is properly sealed, the Instant Pot will indicate so with a brief rising chime. If the sealing is successful, the pot will initiate the selected program and no longer show an error code.

(2) LIQUID AND VOLUME: In order for the pot to pressurize, you need to have liquid—generally about 2 cups—in the inner pot. Recipes will call for the amount of liquid (usually water or broth) needed for a 6-quart pot.

For consistent results, always keep food and liquid contents at or below the markings on the inner pot. For pressure cooking, you should never fill the inner pot past the **PC Max—⅔** indicator imprinted on the inside of the inner pot. For many foods, it's best to keep the volume at or below the **½** mark, particularly for foods that tend to expand in volume, such as beans or pasta.

As a general rule, the more volume you have in the pot, the longer it will take to reach full pressurization and the longer it will take for the pressure to release naturally once the cooking time is complete.

(3) TEMPERATURE: The temperature of foods that you place in the Instant Pot can have a direct impact on the results. Placing cold or frozen foods in the Instant Pot will cause it to take much longer to achieve full pressurization and temperature. You should always consider this when planning your cooking times, and assume that the colder the foods are that you place in the pot, the longer the build times will be. Room temperature foods can also have some impact on build and cooking times.

(4) ALTITUDE: Because you are cooking with pressure, atmospheric pressure can affect total cooking times. For locations below an elevation of 2,000 feet (610m) above sea level, no additional adjustments are necessary; however, for locations at or above 2,000 feet (610m), you should increase the cooking times by 5 percent for every 1,000 feet (300m) at or above the 2,000-foot (610-m) level. Some Instant Pots, such as the Ultra, have an altitude adjustment function built in.

PRESSURE RELEASE

Once the pressure cooking time is complete, you must release the pressure inside the pot before opening the lid. There are two ways to do this. For perfectly cooked food, always use the method called for in the recipe.

(1) NATURAL RELEASE: Natural pressure release begins automatically when a pressure cooking program is completed—or when the **Cancel** button is pressed—as the pot slowly releases steam. This method can take significantly longer than quick pressure release—typically anywhere between 5 to 30 minutes, depending on what is being cooked, the pressure at which it is being cooked, and the volume of food in the pot. When cooking foamy foods or recipes with a large volume, it is a good idea to naturally release the pressure for at least a few minutes to prevent sputtering out of the steam release valve. The gradual natural pressure release is also helpful when cooking dry beans because it helps keep beans intact.

Your food is still cooking while pressure is being naturally released. This cooking time is built into many recipes to achieve the best-cooked results, so don't skip it.

(2) QUICK RELEASE: A quick pressure release is achieved by manually pressing down the **Quick Release** button until it clicks and locks into the venting position, allowing pressure to quickly escape. To stop the quick release, slightly turn the button counterclockwise until it pops up to the sealing position. Quick pressure release is useful for vegetables, pasta, and other foods that can quickly become overcooked. Note that the quick release method should be done with caution, as the pot releases the pressure rapidly and can cause burns; never place your hand or face directly over the vent on the steam release handle. (As an added precaution, you can use a wooden spoon to flip the handle to the venting position.)

Maintenance

The Instant Pot makes cleanup easy because many parts are dishwasher safe. The lid is top-rack dishwasher safe, and the stainless steel inner pot and the sealing ring are also dishwasher safe. The anti-block shield and sealing ring should be removed and washed in hot, soapy water after each use. Never place the base of the Instant Pot in the dishwasher or get the heating element wet. To clean the exterior or lip of the pot, use a damp cloth.

Replacement parts are available and should be purchased whenever you notice cracks or deformations. The sealing ring may need to be replaced every 18 to 24 months because it absorbs cooking odors.

OUTER LID

STEAM RELEASE VALVE: If your lid is in the **Sealing** position, this valve allows a small amount of steam to release while pressure is building. If your lid is in the **Venting** position, it continuously releases steam.

QUICK RELEASE BUTTON: Use this button to control whether the pot is sealed or venting. When in the sealing position, the pot is able to build and maintain pressure. To manually release pressure, press the button down until it clicks into the venting position. Some models have a button that automatically pops up to the sealing position when the lid locks. Others have a steam release switch, which is toggled back and forth.

FLOAT VALVE: The float valve indicates whether the cooking chamber is pressurized. If the valve is raised up, the pot contains pressure—you must release the pressure before you can open the lid. If the float valve is sunken down, the pot is not pressurized. Always make sure the float valve is down before attempting to open the lid.

INNER LID

SEALING RING: You'll notice several components if you flip the lid upside down. The sealing ring is the silicone piece that runs around the perimeter of the lid interior. Without this ring properly in place, the pot can't seal and pressurize.

FLOAT VALVE: The underside of the float valve is covered with a silicone cap. This cap keeps the valve cleared of food debris.

ANTI-BLOCK SHIELD: The round anti-block shield covers the interior side of the steam release valve and prevents food and foam from interfering with steam release. This is an important safety piece because it ensures pressure can release from the valve as needed.

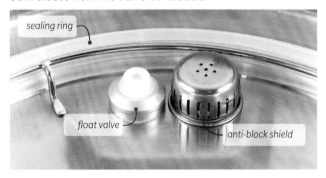

COOKING WITH AN INSTANT POT

The Instant Pot goes far beyond simply pressure cooking. This multi-cooker also sautés, slow cooks, and makes yogurt. Get the most out of your Instant Pot by learning about the various settings, as well as how to use standard and additional accessories.

PRESSURE COOK

This is the setting you'll probably use most often. You can choose **Low** or **High** pressure, as well as the cooking time, on the control panel.

STEAM

The **Steam** setting, which is a pressure cooking function, is a great option for cooking vegetables because it retains more nutrients and color. The recipes in this book use the **High** pressure setting. Use the trivet or steam rack and the quick release method to avoid overcooked veggies.

SLOW COOK

Use the **Low** temperature setting to correspond to a low (8-hour) slow cooker setting; use the **Medium** temperature to correspond to a medium (6-hour) slow cooker setting; use **High** to correspond to a high (4-hour) slow cooker setting. This function is also great for making dry foods such as granola. Make sure the valve is set to the venting position, or use a glass lid, as this is not a pressure function.

SAUTÉ

This is a great way to bring out the flavor of ingredients before pressure cooking, to crisp up foods, to simmer soups, and to reduce sauces. The recipes in this book usually recommend the **Medium** setting, but the **High** setting is useful when boiling down a sauce, and **Low** is useful when cooking foods that can easily burn.

CAKE

This **High** pressure mode creates a very moist, dense cake. The **Low** mode creates a lighter, moister cake.

BEAN/CHILI

If you want firmer-textured beans, use the **High** pressure setting. For softer beans, use the **Low** pressure setting.

RICE

This setting cooks on lower pressure and is best for white, rather than brown rice. For rice with a firmer texture, use the **Low** mode, and for rice with a softer texture, use the **High** mode.

SOUP/BROTH

This program brings soups to a slow simmer and also results in a clear broth. For most vegetable soups, the **Low** setting is best.

YOGURT

The **Medium** mode is used for fermenting milk, while the **High** mode is used for pasteurizing milk. The Easy Vanilla Yogurt Jars (see p26) in this book skip the pasteurizing step.

Pressure Cooking Times

There are several timing components to take into consideration before beginning a recipe.

- **PREP:** The time needed to get all your ingredients ready to cook, such as peeling or chopping.
- **BUILD:** The time it takes the Instant Pot to reach pressure. Your display time will not begin counting down until your pot has reached pressure. The build time can vary depending on a number of factors, including the total volume of food in

the pot, the temperature of the food, atmospheric pressure, and room temperature. As a general rule, recipes take 5 to 15 minutes to come to pressure.

- **PRESSURE:** The cook time you'll be setting on the pot. Keep in mind that the food will also be cooking during the build and any natural release times.
- **RELEASE:** The time it takes to release the pressure from the pot. Once the cook time is complete, the LED display will automatically begin to count upward as the natural release occurs. With the natural release method, the time it takes for the pot to release all pressure will vary greatly depending on the volume

TROUBLESHOOTING

OVERCOOKED VEGETABLES: One of the challenges when starting out with pressure cooking is choosing cook times. To avoid mushy vegetables, err on the lower end of the cook times. You can always lock the lid and cook longer, but you can't "un-cook" an overcooked dish. Remember that cooking begins during the build time and continues through release time. To steam broccoli, for example, I set the pressure cook time to 0 minutes because it cooks perfectly during the build time.

BURN WARNING: This frustrating situation comes about when the pot overheats. Often, ingredients have become stuck to the bottom of the pot during cooking. The Instant Pot will automatically reduce the temperature and may not reach pressure. To avoid this, you must use enough liquid. Try to avoid cooking with very thick liquids, such as tomato sauce. For example, when making the Mexican Rice recipe (see p115), it's crucial to layer the tomatoes on top without stirring so that the rice can cook without the tomatoes burning on the bottom. After sautéing, prevent the burn warning by deglazing the pot and scraping up any bits stuck to the bottom with a spatula.

NOT COMING TO PRESSURE: Check that the valve is set to the sealing position and the sealing ring is properly positioned. The pot also must be filled with enough liquid for pressure to build.

STEAM LEAKING OUT FROM UNDER LID: This is usually a sealing ring issue. Remove the lid and ensure the ring is properly positioned, undamaged, and free of food particles.

of food—usually it's between 5 and 30 minutes. If you use the quick release method, it will only take about 1 minute. Many recipes call for letting the pot naturally release for a specified time before manually releasing any remaining pressure.

- **TOTAL:** The approximate time it will take to make the dish from start to finish. This includes additional preparations after pressure cooking, such as simmering, broiling, roasting, or cooling.

ACCESSORIES

Trivet or steam rack
This accessory comes with the Instant Pot. It raises food or another dish off the bottom of the pot. It's ideal for pot-in-pot cooking (placing a second vessel within the inner pot) and for steaming larger vegetables. Older models come with a trivet, and newer models come with a steam rack with handles.

Springform pan
A springform pan is useful when making cakes, cheesecakes, and casseroles such as lasagna. Look for a 6- to 7-inch (15.25–17.5cm) pan that will fit inside the inner pot.

Steamer basket
This accessory helps to steam food that would otherwise fall through the trivet. Look for a stainless steel or silicone model with legs, which allows steam to circulate. Ensure it's a size that fits in the pot.

Ramekins and Instant Pot-safe bowls
These are useful for pot-in-pot cooking. Ramekins are perfect for individual desserts, such as apple crisp. Larger Instant Pot-safe dishes, such as Pyrex, are ideal for cooking rice and other dishes on the trivet.

Tempered glass lid
A vented glass lid is useful for cooking without pressure, such as during the Slow Cook and Yogurt programs. You can buy an Instant Pot glass lid, but you might already have a standard pot or pan lid that fits the Instant Pot.

YOUR VEGAN PANTRY

Stock your kitchen with whole food staples and you'll be ready to whip up a nutritious meal any time. I love to purchase dry staples from bulk bins and store them in glass jars, which is a more economical and environmentally friendly way to cook. Here are some plant-based staples to get you started.

FRUITS AND VEGETABLES

For the best flavor and price, it's best to use in-season produce. Staples to keep on hand year-round include **onions, garlic, carrots, celery, potatoes, canned** or **boxed tomatoes, fresh spinach** or **kale,** and **fresh herbs.** These ingredients are the base for many one-pot meals. Frozen produce is a nutritious and economical way to enjoy seasonal foods like berries and peaches year-round.

LEGUMES

The Instant Pot shines when it comes to legumes, and it makes switching from canned to dried easy. Some legumes to keep on hand include **green** and **red lentils, chickpeas, black beans, pinto beans, white beans,** and **black-eyed peas.**

GRAINS

Rice and other grains are a great base, side, or ingredient for many plant-based recipes. Stock up on **rolled** and **steel-cut oats, brown** and **white rice, Arborio rice, quinoa, farro, millet,** and **pasta.**

OILS

Those on a strict whole food, plant-based diet do not consume any oils because they are not whole foods. If you would like to cook without oil, you can still use many of the recipes in this cookbook. Simply omit the oil called for in sautéing and dry sauté, or use a splash of water or vegetable broth. If you do use oil, here are some healthy ones to keep on hand: **extra virgin olive oil, coconut oil, sesame oil,** and **avocado oil**.

FLOURS

Almond flour, all-purpose flour, and **whole wheat pastry flour** are the ones I use most often. There are several great **gluten-free, all-purpose flours** on the market today, as well. **Oat flour** is also great for gluten-free baking, and it's easy to make by grinding certified gluten-free oats in a blender.

NUTS AND SEEDS

Nuts and seeds are a good source of plant-based protein and healthy fats; sprinkle them on salads and breakfast bowls. **Almonds, walnuts, raw cashews, flax seeds** or **meal, pepitas, hemp seeds, chia seeds,** and **nut butters** are great to keep in stock.

SWEETENERS

Refined white sugar is not necessary for deliciously sweet treats. Choose instead **pure maple syrup, agave nectar, coconut sugar,** and **organic stevia.**

BROTHS AND STOCKS

Keep several boxes of **vegetable broth** or **stock** in the pantry so you're always ready to make a soup or risotto. You can also make your own broth and store it in the refrigerator or freezer. For rich stews like vegan bourguignon or soup with that classic chicken soup flavor, keep **vegan chicken bouillon** and **vegan beef bouillon** on hand.

MILK ALTERNATIVES

There are many dairy-free milk varieties on the market today: **almond, soy, cashew, oat, flax, hemp, pea,** and more. Try a few to find which you like best. Stick with unsweetened milk alternatives to reduce sugar intake and so that you can control the sweetness by adding your own to taste.

CHEESE ALTERNATIVES

Once soaked, **raw cashews** can be blended into an incredibly creamy sauce and used to make everything from homemade vegan cream cheese, to alfredo sauce and macaroni and cheese. **Raw slivered almonds** work similarly and are wonderful for making vegan ricotta. Store-bought dairy alternatives you may wish to keep in the refrigerator include **vegan butter** such as Miyoko's, **cream cheese** such as Kite Hill, **Parmesan** such as Follow Your Heart, and a **soft artisan cheese** such as Treeline or Miyoko's. **Nutritional yeast** can add the rich umami you'd get from cheese, as well as vitamins and minerals.

EGG REPLACEMENTS

For baking, you can create a vegan "egg" by mixing 1 tablespoon **flax meal** or **chia seeds** with 3 tablespoons water and letting sit until gelled, about 5 minutes. The best commercial egg replacer for baking I've found is **Bob's Red Mill Egg Replacer.** For savory egg-like dishes, **extra-firm tofu** makes a great scramble. **Chickpea flour** bakes up into an incredibly egg-like consistency in omelets, quiches, and frittatas.

BREAKFAST

SERVES: 2

PREP: 5 MINUTES
PRESSURE: 2 MINUTES
TOTAL: 20 MINUTES

 SETTINGS: PRESSURE COOK (HIGH), SAUTÉ (HIGH)
RELEASE: QUICK

2 cups water

2 small Yukon Gold potatoes, cut into 1-in (2.5cm) chunks

2 tbsp extra virgin olive oil

10oz (285g) (about 1½ cups) firm organic tofu, drained and crumbled

½ tsp ground turmeric

2 tbsp nutritional yeast

½ tsp sea salt

Pinch of freshly ground black pepper

¼ cup unsweetened plant-based milk (optional for a softer texture)

2 (10-in; 25cm) flour tortillas, warmed (gluten-free, if needed)

½ avocado, sliced

1 cup fresh baby spinach or arugula

¼ cup salsa

TOFU SCRAMBLE BREAKFAST BURRITO

Warm, filling, and protein-rich breakfast burritos filled with potatoes, tofu scramble, greens, and avocado are a delicious way to start the day or refuel after a workout.

1 Add 2 cups water to the inner pot, and fit with a steamer basket. Place the potato chunks in the steamer basket. Lock the lid and ensure the steam release valve is set to the sealing position. Select **Pressure Cook (High),** and set the cook time for **2 minutes.**

2 Once the cook time is complete, immediately quick release the pressure. Carefully remove the lid and steamer basket. Drain the water from the inner pot and place the pot back into the Instant Pot.

3 Select **Sauté (High),** and heat the oil until very hot. Add the potatoes and cook, turning occasionally, until crisp on the outside, about 3 minutes. Use a spatula to remove the potatoes from the pot and set aside on a plate.

4 Add the crumbled tofu, turmeric, nutritional yeast, salt, and pepper to the pot, and sauté for 1 to 2 minutes until hot. If desired for a softer scramble, add the milk and simmer until warm and the milk has evaporated and absorbed.

5 To assemble the burritos, place the potatoes and tofu scramble on the warm tortillas. Top with equal portions of avocado, greens, and salsa. Roll into burritos and enjoy immediately.

tip *This recipe makes 2 breakfast burritos, but you can halve the ingredients for one serving.*

Nutrition per serving:
CALORIES: 686; **TOTAL FAT:** 31g; **SATURATED FAT:** 4g; **CHOLESTEROL:** 0mg; **SODIUM:** 971mg; **TOTAL CARBOHYDRATE:** 74g; **FIBER:** 14g; **PROTEIN:** 26g

SERVES: 4

PREP: 5 MINUTES
PRESSURE: 27 MINUTES
TOTAL: 45 MINUTES

SETTINGS: SAUTÉ (MEDIUM), PRESSURE COOK (HIGH)
RELEASE: NATURAL, QUICK

2 tsp extra virgin olive oil, divided

½ yellow onion, diced

2 cups water

½ cup dry black beans, rinsed

1 chipotle pepper in adobo sauce

½ tsp garlic powder

¾ tsp sea salt, plus more to taste

1 tsp adobo sauce

8oz (225g) extra-firm tofu, drained

Pinch of ground turmeric

8 small corn tortillas, warmed in the microwave or lightly charred in a skillet

1 cup baby spinach

1 avocado, sliced

1 cup pico de gallo

2 radishes, thinly sliced

1 cup fresh cilantro

CHIPOTLE HUEVOS-LESS RANCHEROS

This lighter take on the favorite Mexican brunch is made with smoky, spicy chipotle black bean tofu scramble and plenty of fresh toppings.

1 Select **Sauté (Medium),** and heat 1 teaspoon oil (optional), in the inner pot until hot. (Otherwise, you can dry sauté in the hot pot or add a bit of water in the bottom of the pot.) Add the onion and sauté until softened and golden, 3 to 5 minutes. Press **Cancel.** Add 2 cups water, beans, chipotle pepper, and garlic powder.

2 Lock the lid and ensure the steam release valve is set to the sealing position. Select **Pressure Cook (High),** and set the cook time for **27 minutes.**

3 Once the cook time is complete, allow the pressure to release naturally for 10 minutes, then quick release any remaining pressure. Carefully remove the lid. Stir in the salt, and remove and discard the chipotle pepper. Transfer to a medium bowl. Add the adobo sauce ¼ tsp at a time to add heat to taste, if desired.

4 Rinse out the inner pot and place back into the Instant Pot. Select **Sauté (High),** and heat the remaining 1 teaspoon oil. Pat the tofu with paper towels to soak up as much water as possible. Crumble the tofu into the pot with the hot oil. Season with turmeric and salt. Sauté until hot, about 2 minutes. Drain the beans and add them into the tofu scramble, or keep them separate. Press **Cancel.**

5 To assemble the dish, place the warm tortillas on plates. Top with a few spinach leaves and the bean and tofu scramble, avocado, pico de gallo, radish, and cilantro. Enjoy immediately.

tip *For a soy-free option, skip the tofu scramble and top with vegan sour cream.*

Nutrition per serving:
CALORIES: 335; **TOTAL FAT:** 12g; **SATURATED FAT:** 2g; **CHOLESTEROL:** 0mg; **SODIUM:** 578mg; **TOTAL CARBOHYDRATE:** 45g; **FIBER:** 10g; **PROTEIN:** 14g

VEGGIE HASH

A big bowl of veggies has never tasted so good. Feel free to get creative and use whatever veggies you have—cherry tomatoes, corn, quartered Brussels sprouts, chard, and kale are all fantastic additions to a potato hash.

SERVES: 6

PREP: 5 MINUTES
PRESSURE: 2 MINUTES
TOTAL: 30 MINUTES

SETTINGS: PRESSURE COOK (HIGH)
RELEASE: NATURAL, QUICK

1 Fit the inner pot with a steamer basket and add 1 cup water. Add the potatoes to the steamer basket. Lock the lid and ensure the steam release valve is set to the sealing position. Select **Pressure Cook (High),** and set the cook time for **2 minutes.**

2 Once the cook time is complete, allow the pressure to release naturally for 5 minutes, then quick release any remaining pressure. Carefully remove the lid and make sure the potatoes are fork tender. If not, lock the lid and pressure cook for 1 minute more until tender. Remove the steamer basket.

3 While the potatoes are cooking, in a large cast-iron skillet, heat 1 tablespoon oil over medium-high heat. Add the onion and sauté until softened and golden, 3 to 5 minutes. Add the bell pepper, mushrooms, and zucchini, and sauté until tender, about 4 minutes more. Season with paprika, garlic powder, salt, and pepper. Transfer the veggies to another dish, and set aside. Clean out the skillet and return it to the stove.

4 Add the remaining 3 tablespoons oil to the skillet, and turn the heat to high, or select **Sauté (High)** and use the Instant Pot. When the oil is hot, add the steamed potatoes in a single layer, working in batches as needed. Let cook 1 minute until browned on the bottom, then flip. Continue cooking until the potatoes are browned on all sides, turning and adding more oil as needed. It's okay if some pieces get stuck to the bottom—try to scrape up stuck pieces with a metal spatula.

5 Add the kale or spinach and the sautéed veggies. Toss to wilt the greens. Season to taste with additional salt and pepper. Garnish with fresh basil and serve immediately.

1 cup water

4 cups (1-in; 2.5cm) russet potato cubes (about 2 potatoes)

4 tbsp extra virgin olive oil, divided

1 small yellow onion, diced

1 red bell pepper, deseeded and diced

8oz (225g) sliced baby bella mushrooms

1 zucchini, diced

1 tsp paprika

1 tsp garlic powder

Sea salt, to taste

Freshly ground black pepper, to taste

2 cups roughly chopped curly kale or spinach

½ cup fresh basil, thinly sliced

tip *You can make this dish entirely in the Instant Pot by cooking the vegetables on Sauté (High), but it's much quicker to sauté the vegetables on the stove while the potatoes are steaming in the Instant Pot. Whether you're making french fries or breakfast hash, the secret to potatoes that are fluffy on the inside and crispy on the outside is steaming, then frying in plenty of oil over high heat.*

Nutrition per serving:
CALORIES: 191; **TOTAL FAT:** 10g; **SATURATED FAT:** 1g; **CHOLESTEROL:** 0mg;
SODIUM: 91mg; **TOTAL CARBOHYDRATE:** 24g; **FIBER:** 4g; **PROTEIN:** 5g

LEEK, ASPARAGUS, AND SPINACH FRITTATA

This savory breakfast or brunch recipe is great for those times you're craving fresh green vegetables. Chickpea flour imparts a soft egg-like texture, and the leek and asparagus add a tender-crisp crunch.

 SERVES: 6

 PREP: 10 MINUTES
PRESSURE: 8 MINUTES
TOTAL: 25 MINUTES

 SETTINGS: SAUTÉ (HIGH), PRESSURE COOK (HIGH)
RELEASE: QUICK

1 Coat a 7 inch (17.5cm) springform pan with cooking spray, or brush with olive oil. Set aside. In a medium mixing bowl, whisk together the chickpea flour, baking powder, garlic powder, salt, and pepper. Add 1⅛ cup water, vinegar, and mustard, and whisk vigorously until bubbly and well combined, about 1 minute. Set aside.

2 Select **Sauté (High),** and heat the oil in the inner pot, or use a medium skillet over medium-high heat. Sauté the leeks and asparagus with a pinch of salt and pepper until the asparagus is just tender, about 5 minutes. Add the spinach and sauté until wilted, about 1 minute.

3 Evenly spread the vegetables in the springform pan. If you used the inner pot to sauté, clean it out and place back in the Instant Pot. Pour the chickpea flour mixture over the vegetables. Cover the top of the pan with foil.

4 Fit the inner pot with the trivet or steam rack, and add the remaining 1 cup water. Place the pan on the trivet. Lock the lid and ensure the steam release valve is set to the sealing position. Select **Pressure Cook (High),** and set the cook time for **8 minutes.**

5 Once the cook time is complete, immediately quick release the pressure. Carefully remove the lid and the pan. Remove the foil and let the pan rest on a cooling rack for 5 minutes.

6 Use a thin knife, if needed, to release the frittata from the sides of the pan. Remove the sides of the pan. If desired, place on a cookie sheet and broil for a few minutes to brown the top.

7 Cut into slices and serve immediately, garnished with chives and yogurt or cheese, if desired. This recipe is best served right when it's made because the frittata will become more dense the longer it sits.

1 cup chickpea flour (also called garbanzo bean or gram flour)

1 tsp baking powder

1 tsp garlic powder

½ tsp sea salt

¼ tsp freshly ground black pepper

2⅛ cups water, divided

¼ tsp apple cider vinegar

1 tsp Dijon mustard

1 tbsp extra virgin olive oil

1 cup chopped leeks (about 1 leek)

1 cup (2-in; 5cm) asparagus pieces (about ½ of a bunch)

1 cup packed baby spinach

¼ cup chopped chives, for garnish

6oz (170g) plain dairy-free yogurt (such as Kite Hill) or soft cheese (such as Miyoko's or Treeline) (optional), for garnish

tip *Chickpea flour is commonly used in Italian and French recipes like socca or farinata; in Indian cooking, where it's known as gram flour; and in gluten-free baking. Find chickpea flour in natural foods stores, online, or at Indian markets.*

Nutrition per serving:
CALORIES: 98; **TOTAL FAT:** 3g; **SATURATED FAT:** 0g **CHOLESTEROL:** 0mg; **SODIUM:** 284mg; **TOTAL CARBOHYDRATE:** 13g; **FIBER:** 3g; **PROTEIN:** 4g

SERVES: 2

 PREP: 2 MINUTES
PRESSURE: 12 MINUTES
TOTAL: 30 MINUTES

 SETTINGS: PRESSURE COOK (HIGH)
RELEASE: NATURAL, QUICK

1 medium sweet potato

1 cup water

Pinch of ground cinnamon

2 tbsp almond butter

¼ cup slivered almonds, toasted

2 tbsp hemp seeds

LOADED BREAKFAST SWEET POTATO

This naturally sweet breakfast is warm and filling. The soft sweet potato gets just the right amount of crunch from the toasted almonds and hemp seeds.

1 Wash and dry the sweet potato. Pierce all over with a fork. Fit the inner pot with the trivet or steam rack, and add 1 cup water. Place the sweet potato on the trivet.

2 Lock the lid and ensure the steam release valve is set to the sealing position. Select **Pressure Cook (High),** and set the cook time for **12 minutes.**

3 Once the cook time is complete, allow the pressure to release naturally for 10 minutes, then quick release any remaining pressure. Carefully remove the lid and make sure the sweet potato is fork-tender. If not, lock the lid and pressure cook for 3 minutes more, or until tender.

4 Carefully remove the potato with tongs. Cut in half lengthwise and place on two serving plates. Top with a pinch of cinnamon and a drizzle of almond butter. Sprinkle almonds and hemp seeds on top. Serve warm.

tip *Swap in any variety of your favorite nut butter, and add additional toppings, such as sliced bananas or berries. To make this dish nut-free, use sunflower seed butter.*

Nutrition per serving:
CALORIES: 312; **TOTAL FAT:** 20g; **SATURATED FAT:** 2g; **CHOLESTEROL:** 0mg; **SODIUM:** 55mg; **TOTAL CARBOHYDRATE:** 28g; **FIBER:** 7g; **PROTEIN:** 11g

LOWER-SUGAR STRAWBERRY CHIA JAM

This lower-sugar jam uses maple syrup as an unrefined sweetener. It is easy to make, and it tastes wonderful on toast with almond butter, on pancakes, in oatmeal, or in breakfast quinoa.

 MAKES: ABOUT 1½ CUPS

 PREP: 2 MINUTES
PRESSURE: 1 MINUTE
TOTAL: 25 MINUTES

 SETTINGS: PRESSURE COOK (HIGH), SAUTÉ (MEDIUM)
RELEASE: NATURAL

12oz (340g) fresh or frozen strawberries

2 tbsp fresh lemon juice

1 tbsp pure maple syrup

1 tbsp water

1 tbsp arrowroot starch

1 tbsp chia seeds

1 Add the strawberries, lemon juice, and maple syrup to the inner pot. Lock the lid and ensure the steam release valve is set to the sealing position. Select **Pressure Cook (High),** and set the cook time for **1 minute.**

2 Once the cook time is complete, allow the pressure to release naturally. Carefully remove the lid—it will look very watery with soft strawberries. Mash the strawberries with a wooden spoon.

3 Make a slurry by whisking together 1 tablespoon water and arrowroot in a small bowl. Stir the slurry into the pot. Simmer on **Sauté (Medium)** until thickened, 2 to 3 minutes, stirring with a wooden spoon. Stir in the chia seeds.

4 Transfer the jam to a glass storage container and let cool to room temperature. Secure the lid and store in the refrigerator for up to 5 days.

tip *Add more sweetness with an extra splash of maple syrup or a few drops of liquid stevia to taste.*

Nutrition per tablespoon:
CALORIES: 12; **TOTAL FAT:** 0g; **SATURATED FAT:** 0g; **CHOLESTEROL:** 0mg; **SODIUM:** 0mg; **TOTAL CARBOHYDRATE:** 3g; **FIBER:** 0g; **PROTEIN:** 0g

SERVES: 4

 PREP: 5 MINUTES
PRESSURE: 18 HOURS
TOTAL: 20 HOURS

 SETTINGS: YOGURT (MEDIUM)
RELEASE: NONE

4 cups plain soy or pea-based milk (recommended WestSoy, Trader Joe's Organic Soy Beverage, or Ripple)

1 (5oz; 140g) container plain or vanilla vegan yogurt with live cultures (such as Silk or Kite Hill)

2 tsp vanilla bean paste, or seeds from 1 vanilla bean

Organic liquid stevia (optional), to taste

EASY VANILLA YOGURT JARS

Thick, rich, and creamy homemade vanilla bean yogurt tastes so much better than store-bought. Top with berries and Crunchy Granola (see p28) for a delicious and nutritious grab-and-go breakfast.

1 Pour the milk and yogurt into a medium bowl. Whisk until completely combined. Whisk in the vanilla bean paste or seeds. If desired, sweeten to taste with a few drops of liquid stevia.

2 Pour the milk mixture evenly into 4 pint-sized glass jars. Place the jars directly into the inner pot, not on a trivet. (You won't need any water in the pot because it is not using pressure.)

3 Place the glass lid on top of the Instant Pot, or use your regular lid with the steam release valve in the venting position. Select **Yogurt (Medium),** and set the cook time for **18 hours.** Your yogurt is ready when it's thick; this may take anywhere from 13 to 20 hours. Once the yogurt is the desired consistency, remove the jars and secure with the lids. Store in the refrigerator for up to 1 week.

4 Enjoy your homemade yogurt cold. The top half of each jar will be empty and ready to be filled with your favorite fruit or granola and a splash of maple syrup.

tip *For future batches of yogurt, there's no need to buy commercial yogurt because you can use your homemade yogurt as the starter!*

Not all plant-based milks work for this easy yogurt recipe. It's important to use a higher-protein milk like soy or pea milk. The brands that work best are WestSoy or Trader Joe's Organic Soy Beverage cartons and Ripple. Natural almond and coconut milk beverages will result in runny yogurt that never sets up.

Nutrition per serving:
CALORIES: 158; **TOTAL FAT:** 4g; **SATURATED FAT:** 1g; **CHOLESTEROL:** 0mg; **SODIUM:** 96mg; **TOTAL CARBOHYDRATE:** 25g; **FIBER:** 1g; **PROTEIN:** 9g

CRUNCHY GRANOLA

 MAKES: ABOUT 3½ CUPS

 PREP: 10 MINUTES
PRESSURE: 4 HOURS
TOTAL: 5 HOURS

 SETTINGS: SLOW COOK (LOW)
RELEASE: NONE

1 cup old-fashioned rolled oats (certified gluten-free, if needed)

½ cup raw, hulled sunflower seeds

½ cup raw, hulled pepitas (pumpkin seeds)

½ cup raw pecans, roughly chopped

⅓ cup hemp seeds

½ tsp ground cinnamon

1 tsp coconut sugar

⅛ tsp sea salt

2½ tbsp melted coconut oil, plus more to grease

2½ tbsp pure maple syrup

Lightly sweet, this crunchy granola is filled with nourishing seeds and nuts. It makes an excellent breakfast or snack with yogurt or almond milk and berries.

1 Lightly rub the bottom of the inner pot with a little bit of coconut oil or lightly coat with cooking spray.

2 In a medium bowl, mix the oats, sunflower seeds, pepitas, pecans, hemp seeds, cinnamon, coconut sugar, and salt.

3 Drizzle the coconut oil and maple syrup over the granola mixture. Toss with your hands or a spatula until well combined.

4 Transfer the mixture to the inner pot. Partially cover the Instant Pot with a glass lid, if you have one, or use the standard lid with the steam release valve set to the venting position. Select **Slow Cook (Low),** and set the cook time for **4 hours.** Stir halfway through, and slow cook until crunchy. Press **Cancel.**

5 Let the granola cool completely in the pot, and then stir. Transfer to a lidded storage container, and store for up to 1 week at room temperature.

tip *Feel free to use whatever nuts and seeds you have on hand. Coconut is a nice addition, as well.*

Nutrition per ¼ cup:
CALORIES: 155; **TOTAL FAT:** 12g; **SATURATED FAT:** 3g; **CHOLESTEROL:** 0mg; **SODIUM:** 12mg; **TOTAL CARBOHYDRATE:** 9g; **FIBER:** 2g; **PROTEIN:** 5g

STONE FRUIT COMPOTE

This beautiful fruit recipe is a great way to use up late-summer peaches, plums, or apricots. It tastes like pie filling and is cooked with only 1 minute of pressure time. Serve on waffles or pancakes or with yogurt.

MAKES: ABOUT 2 CUPS

PREP: 5 MINUTES
PRESSURE: 1 MINUTE
TOTAL: 25 MINUTES

SETTINGS: PRESSURE COOK (HIGH), SAUTÉ (HIGH)
RELEASE: NATURAL

1   In the inner pot, stir together all ingredients. Lock the lid and ensure the steam release valve is set to the sealing position. Select **Pressure Cook (High),** and set the cook time for **1 minute.**

2   Once the cook time is complete, allow the pressure to release naturally. Carefully remove the lid and select **Sauté (High).** Simmer for 2 minutes to thicken. Press **Cancel.** Taste and add additional syrup or cinnamon, if desired. Serve warm. Store in an airtight container in the refrigerator for up to 1 week.

4 cups sliced stone fruit (plums, apricots, or peaches)

1 tbsp fresh lemon juice

1 tbsp pure maple syrup or agave nectar

½ tsp vanilla bean paste or extract

Pinch of ground cinnamon

⅛ cup water

tip *There is no need to peel the fruit—the skins add great flavor and texture. When stone fruit isn't in season, you can use a bag of frozen sliced peaches in this recipe.*

Nutrition per ¼ cup:
CALORIES: 37; **TOTAL FAT:** 0g; **SATURATED FAT:** 0g; **CHOLESTEROL:** 0mg; **SODIUM:** 0mg; **TOTAL CARBOHYDRATE:** 9g; **FIBER:** 1g; **PROTEIN:** 1g

SERVES: 4

 PREP: 2 MINUTES
PRESSURE: 12 MINUTES
TOTAL: 30 MINUTES

 SETTINGS: PRESSURE COOK (HIGH)
RELEASE: NATURAL, QUICK

1 cup millet

1 cup water

2 cups plant-based milk, divided, plus more for serving

½ tsp pure vanilla extract

½ tsp ground cinnamon

1 tbsp vegan butter

1 tbsp coconut sugar

2 bananas, peeled and quartered (cut in half lengthwise, then crosswise)

Pure maple syrup, to taste

½ cup slivered almonds, lightly toasted

BANANAS FOSTER MILLET BOWL

Warm, caramelized bananas top millet porridge bowls for a deliciously satisfying breakfast. Vanilla and cinnamon impart a sweet, pleasant aroma and flavor.

1 In the inner pot, stir together the millet, 1 cup water, 1 cup milk, vanilla, and cinnamon. Lock the lid and ensure the steam release valve is set to the sealing position. Select **Pressure Cook (High),** and set the cook time for **12 minutes.**

2 Once the cook time is complete, allow the pressure to release naturally for 10 minutes, then quick release any remaining pressure. Carefully remove the lid and stir in the remaining 1 cup milk. Select **Warm** while cooking the bananas.

3 In a medium frying pan, melt the butter over medium heat. Whisk in the coconut sugar. Place the bananas cut-side down into the butter and sugar. Cook, turning once, until caramelized, about 3 minutes total.

4 Serve the millet porridge in bowls and top with the bananas, maple syrup, more milk, and slivered almonds. Enjoy immediately.

tip *Feel free to add any other fruit, seeds, and nuts you like to this bowl. Raspberries and hemp seeds go especially well.*

Nutrition per serving (with 1 tsp maple syrup):
CALORIES: 408; **TOTAL FAT:** 13g; **SATURATED FAT:** 2g; **CHOLESTEROL:** 0mg;
SODIUM: 97mg; **TOTAL CARBOHYDRATE:** 63g; **FIBER:** 8g; **PROTEIN:** 10g

CHOCOLATE STEEL-CUT OATS

Chocolate for breakfast? Heck, yes! This warm, nourishing bowl of chocolate oats is sure get the day started on a happy note. Topped with fresh fruit, it's full of a variety of flavors and textures.

 SERVES: 4

 PREP: 3 MINUTES
PRESSURE: 4 MINUTES
TOTAL. 35 MINUTES

 SETTINGS: PRESSURE COOK (HIGH)
RELEASE: NATURAL, QUICK

1 Add all of the ingredients, except toppings, to the inner pot, and whisk to combine. Lock the lid and ensure the steam release valve is set to the sealing position. Select **Pressure Cook (High),** and set the cook time for **4 minutes.**

2 Once the cook time is complete, allow the pressure to release naturally for 15 minutes, then quick release any remaining pressure. Carefully remove the lid and stir the oats. They will thicken up more as they cool.

3 Serve the oats warm in bowls, and top with banana and strawberry slices, a drizzle of almond butter, and a splash of maple syrup.

1 cup steel-cut oats (certified gluten-free, if needed)

3 cups water

¼ tsp sea salt

3 tbsp unsweetened cocoa powder

2 tbsp pure maple syrup

FOR TOPPING:

1 banana, sliced

1 cup sliced strawberries

4 tbsp natural almond butter or peanut butter

Pure maple syrup

tip Oats are naturally gluten-free, but they're often contaminated during processing. Always look for certified gluten-free oats if you have a gluten sensitivity.

Nutrition per serving (including toppings):
CALORIES: 252; **TOTAL FAT:** 9g; **SATURATED FAT:** 1g; **CHOLESTEROL:** 0mg;
SODIUM: 73mg; **TOTAL CARBOHYDRATE:** 22g; **FIBER:** 4g; **PROTEIN:** 5g

QUINOA BREAKFAST BOWLS

Enjoy this warm and hearty breakfast bowl loaded with flavorful toppings. The quinoa is perfectly cooked with the Instant Pot, having just the right amount of bite to contrast the toasted almonds.

1 In the inner pot, stir together the quinoa, almond milk, vanilla, and cinnamon. Lock the lid and ensure the steam release valve is set to the sealing position. Select **Pressure Cook (High),** and set the cook time for **5 minutes.**

2 Once the cook time is complete, immediately quick release the pressure. Carefully remove the lid.

3 If desired, stir in more milk to thin into a porridge. Serve warm in bowls, sweetened to taste with maple syrup and topped generously with fruit and almonds.

 SERVES: 4

 PREP: 5 MINUTES
PRESSURE: 5 MINUTES
TOTAL: 20 MINUTES

 SETTINGS: PRESSURE COOK (HIGH)
RELEASE: QUICK

1 cup quinoa, rinsed and drained

1½ cups unsweetened almond or other plant-based milk, plus more to serve

½ tsp pure vanilla extract

Pinch of ground cinnamon

FOR SERVING:

¼ cup pure maple syrup

1 cup berries (any combination of blueberries, raspberries, or strawberries)

1 banana, sliced

½ cup slivered almonds, toasted

tip *Use this recipe as a canvas for your favorite toppings. It's also great with Stone Fruit Compote (see p29).*

Nutrition per serving (including toppings and ⅛ cup more almond milk):
CALORIES: 321; **TOTAL FAT:** 11g; **SATURATED FAT:** 1g; **CHOLESTEROL:** 0mg;
SODIUM: 80mg; **TOTAL CARBOHYDRATE:** 48g; **FIBER:** 6g; **PROTEIN:** 10g

SERVES: 4

 PREP: 5 MINUTES
PRESSURE: 25 MINUTES
TOTAL: 40 MINUTES

 SETTINGS: PRESSURE COOK (HIGH)
RELEASE: QUICK

1½ cups old-fashioned rolled oats (certified gluten-free, if needed)

⅓ cup coconut sugar

1 tsp baking powder

1 tsp ground cinnamon

1 tbsp flax meal

1 cup almond milk

1 tsp pure vanilla extract

1 tsp freshly grated orange zest

¼ cup applesauce

¾ cup fresh blueberries

1 cup water

⅓ cup slivered almonds, toasted

BLUEBERRY BAKED OATMEAL

Like a cross between a bowl of oatmeal and a muffin, this lightly sweetened and baked oatmeal is loaded with bursts of blueberry, making it a satisfying warm breakfast.

1 In a medium bowl, stir together the oats, coconut sugar, baking powder, cinnamon, and flax meal.

2 Stir in the almond milk, vanilla, orange zest, and applesauce. Fold in the blueberries. Spoon the oat mixture into 4 ramekins. Cover each ramekin tightly with foil.

3 Fit the inner pot with the trivet or steam rack, and add 1 cup water. Place the ramekins on the trivet. Lock the lid and ensure the steam release valve is set to the sealing position. Select **Pressure Cook (High),** and set the cook time for **25 minutes.**

4 Once the cook time is complete, immediately quick release the pressure and carefully remove the lid. Using potholders, remove the ramekins and remove the foil.

5 Sprinkle the top of the oatmeal cups with almonds. Let cool for a few minutes, then serve warm.

Nutrition per serving:
CALORIES: 267; **TOTAL FAT:** 7g; **SATURATED FAT:** 1g; **CHOLESTEROL:** 0mg; **SODIUM:** 78mg; **TOTAL CARBOHYDRATE:** 46g; **FIBER:** 6g; **PROTEIN:** 7g

HOT CHOCOLATE

Lower-sugar homemade hot chocolate is ready in minutes and stays warm for hours in the Instant Pot. It's also delicious when served cold.

 SERVES: 3 (MAKES ABOUT 3 CUPS)

 PREP: 2 MINUTES
PRESSURE: 5 MINUTES
TOTAL: 7 MINUTES

 SETTINGS: SAUTÉ (MEDIUM), WARM (LOW)
RELEASE: NONE

1   Add all ingredients to the inner pot and select **Sauté (Medium).** Whisk continuously until combined and steaming hot. Taste a cooled spoonful, and add more maple syrup, cocoa powder, and chocolate chips as desired for a sweeter or darker blend. Press **Cancel.**

2   Set the Instant Pot to **Warm (Low).** Ladle the warm hot chocolate from the inner pot into mugs and enjoy with a dollop of dairy-free whipped cream, if desired. Store leftovers in the refrigerator for up to 5 days.

3 cups Almond Milk (see p157)

½ tsp pure vanilla extract

1–2 tbsp unsweetened cocoa powder

Pinch of sea salt

1 tbsp pure maple syrup

1–2 tbsp dairy-free dark chocolate chips

Dairy-free whipped cream, to serve

tip *This recipe works perfectly with 1 batch of Almond Milk (see p157), but feel free to double this recipe when serving guests or larger groups. You can also use any store-bought, unsweetened plant-based milk here.*

Nutrition per serving:
CALORIES: 125; **TOTAL FAT:** 8g; **SATURATED FAT:** 1g; **CHOLESTEROL:** 0mg; **SODIUM:** 79mg; **TOTAL CARBOHYDRATE:** 10g; **FIBER:** 3g; **PROTEIN:** 4g

ENTRÉES, SOUPS & STEWS

SERVES: 4

 PREP: 10 MINUTES
PRESSURE: 5 MINUTES
TOTAL: 30 MINUTES

 SETTINGS: SAUTÉ (MEDIUM),
PRESSURE COOK (HIGH)
RELEASE: NATURAL, QUICK

FOR THE JACKFRUIT:

2 (20oz; 570g) cans green jackfruit in brine or water

1 tbsp extra virgin olive oil (optional)

1 yellow onion, diced

4 cloves garlic, minced

1 cup vegetable broth

1 tbsp taco seasoning

1 tsp ground cumin

1 tbsp coconut sugar

¼ tsp sea salt

FOR THE GUACAMOLE:

2 ripe avocados, pitted

Juice of 1 lime

½ jalapeño, deseeded and finely chopped

1 small shallot, finely chopped

2 tbsp chopped cilantro

⅛ tsp sea salt

FOR SERVING:

1 package corn tortillas, warmed (gluten-free, if needed)

1 cup shredded cabbage

½ small red onion, thinly sliced

2 radishes, thinly sliced

Freshly chopped cilantro

JACKFRUIT TACOS
with Guacamole

Mildly spicy jackfruit filling—similar to shredded chicken in texture—makes a great base for veggie tacos. Serve with a side of Fat-Free Refried Beans (see p114) for a delicious Mexican-inspired meal.

1 Drain and rinse the jackfruit in a colander. Pat with a paper towel to remove some of the excess water. Cut the jackfruit into ½-inch (1.25cm) pieces going with the direction of the fibers, from the core outward.

2 Select **Sauté (Medium),** and heat the oil, if using, in the inner pot until hot. (Otherwise, you can dry sauté in the hot pot or add a bit of water in the bottom of the pot.) Add the onion and sauté until softened and golden, 3 to 5 minutes. Add the garlic and sauté for 1 minute more. Add the broth to deglaze the pan, scraping up any bits stuck to the bottom.

3 Place the jackfruit pieces on top of the broth. Sprinkle with taco seasoning, cumin, coconut sugar, and salt. Lock the lid and ensure the steam release valve is set to the sealing position. Select **Pressure Cook (High),** and set the cook time for **5 minutes.**

4 Once the cook time is complete, allow the pressure to release naturally for 3 minutes, then quick release any remaining pressure. Carefully remove the lid. Use a potato masher to smash the jackfruit into stringy, bite-sized pieces. Adjust with salt or taco seasoning to taste. The filling will be soft and moist; if you'd like to dry it out a bit, select **Sauté (High)** and cook for about 2 minutes until some juices have evaporated.

5 Meanwhile, make the guacamole. In a small bowl, mash the avocados. Stir in the remaining ingredients. Taste and add more salt and lime juice, if desired.

6 To assemble each taco, top a warm tortilla with the jackfruit filling, a generous dollop of guacamole, cabbage, red onion, a few radish slices, and fresh cilantro. Serve immediately.

tip *You may notice seeds in your jackfruit. Though some people discard them, they are edible.*

Nutrition per 2 tacos:
CALORIES: 565; **TOTAL FAT:** 17g; **SATURATED FAT:** 2g; **CHOLESTEROL:** 0mg; **SODIUM:** 609mg; **TOTAL CARBOHYDRATE:** 102g; **FIBER:** 13g; **PROTEIN:** 10g

ENCHILADA BAKE

SERVES: 4

PREP: 5 MINUTES
PRESSURE: 25 MINUTES
TOTAL: 1 HOUR

SETTINGS: SAUTÉ (MEDIUM), PRESSURE COOK (HIGH)
RELEASE: QUICK

1 tbsp extra virgin olive oil (optional)

½ yellow onion, cut into ¼-in (0.5cm) slices

1 red bell pepper, deseeded and cut into ¼-in (0.5cm) slices

1 yellow bell pepper, deseeded and cut into ¼-in (0.5cm) slices

Sea salt, to taste

Freshly ground black pepper, to taste

¾ cup red enchilada sauce (gluten-free, if needed), divided

2 cups cooked black beans, drained

6 (6-in; 5.25cm) corn tortillas

½ cup vegan Cheddar cheese shreds (such as So Delicious or Daiya)

1 cup water

½ cup fresh cilantro leaves, for serving

1 avocado, sliced, for serving

Enchiladas are easier than ever in the Instant Pot. This layered casserole features peppers, onions, and black beans, with a vegan cheesy topping and satisfying avocado.

1 Select **Sauté (Medium),** and heat the oil, if using, in the inner pot until hot. (Otherwise, you can dry sauté in the hot pot or add a bit of water in the bottom of the pot.) Add the onion and peppers and season with salt and pepper. Sauté until softened and golden, 5 to 10 minutes. Press **Cancel** and transfer the veggies to a plate. Rinse the inner pot and place back in the Instant Pot.

2 Coat the bottom of a 7-inch (17.5cm) springform pan with ¼ cup enchilada sauce. Cover the sauce with tortillas, tearing as needed to fit. Overlapping a little is okay.

3 Top the tortillas with 1 cup beans in an even layer. Top the beans with a layer of half of the cooked onions and peppers.

4 Top the peppers and onions with another layer of tortillas, tearing as needed, then another ¼ cup sauce, 1 cup beans, and the remaining peppers and onions.

5 Finally, top the second layer of peppers with a third layer of tortillas and the remaining ¼ cup sauce. Sprinkle the cheese evenly over the top of the sauce.

6 Wrap the whole springform pan, under and over, with foil. Fit the inner pot with the trivet or steam rack, and add 1 cup water. Place the foil-wrapped pan onto the trivet. Lock the lid and ensure the steam release valve is set to the sealing position. Select **Pressure Cook (High),** and set the cook time for **25 minutes.**

7 Once the cook time is complete, immediately quick release the pressure and carefully remove the lid. Remove the pan and discard the foil. Let the enchilada bake cool for 10 minutes. Cut into quarters and serve garnished with cilantro and avocado slices.

tip *This recipe is a great way to use leftover Cuban Black Beans (see p62).*

Nutrition per serving:
CALORIES: 360; **TOTAL FAT:** 14g; **SATURATED FAT:** 3g; **CHOLESTEROL:** 0mg; **SODIUM:** 878mg; **TOTAL CARBOHYDRATE:** 51g; **FIBER:** 15g; **PROTEIN:** 11g

EASY BEAN AND RICE BURRITOS

With similar cook times, dried black beans and brown rice can easily be pressure cooked simultaneously using the pot-in-pot method so you have homemade burritos on the table in record time.

 SERVES: 6

 PREP: 5 MINUTES
PRESSURE: 25 MINUTES
TOTAL: 1 HOUR

 SETTINGS: PRESSURE COOK (HIGH)
RELEASE: NATURAL

1 To make the black beans, in the inner pot, add the beans, 2½ cups water, cumin, oregano, and garlic powder, and stir to combine. Do not add the salt to beans until after cooking to prevent toughness. Place the trivet over the beans.

2 Prepare the brown rice. In an oven-safe bowl or baking dish, such as Pyrex, add the rice, 1 cup water, and salt. Place the dish on the trivet.

3 Lock the lid and ensure the steam release valve is set to the sealing position. Select **Pressure Cook (High),** and set the cook time for **25 minutes.**

4 Once the cook time is complete, allow the pressure to release naturally for 15 minutes, then quick release any remaining pressure. Carefully remove the lid. With oven mitts, carefully take the dish of rice off the trivet and remove the trivet. Season the beans with salt to taste. Squeeze the lime juice over the beans and rice.

5 To assemble each burrito, spoon the rice, beans, guacamole, lettuce, cilantro, and hot sauce or salsa (if using) onto a tortilla. Roll up and enjoy immediately.

tip *Add your favorite veggies to these simple burritos. Roasted sweet potatoes or grilled summer vegetables work wonderfully. For spicy beans, toss in 1 chipotle pepper in adobo sauce before cooking.*

Juice of 1 lime

1 cup homemade or store-bought guacamole

1 small head romaine lettuce, chopped

½ cup fresh cilantro leaves (optional)

Hot sauce or fresh salsa (optional)

6 flour tortillas (gluten-free, if needed), warmed

FOR THE BLACK BEANS:

1 cup dried black beans, picked over and rinsed

2½ cups water

1 tsp ground cumin

1 tsp dried oregano

½ tsp garlic powder

Sea salt, to taste

FOR THE BROWN RICE:

1 cup long-grain brown rice, rinsed

1 cup water

Pinch of sea salt

Nutrition per serving:
CALORIES: 462; **TOTAL FAT:** 10g; **SATURATED FAT:** 3g; **CHOLESTEROL:** 0mg; **SODIUM:** 645mg; **TOTAL CARBOHYDRATE:** 75g; **FIBER:** 10g; **PROTEIN:** 15g

PORTOBELLO MUSHROOM BURGERS

These juicy burgers have all the classic flavor and texture you'd expect from a burger. Cooking Portobello mushrooms in the Instant Pot makes homemade veggie burgers easier than ever.

 SERVES: 4

 PREP: 15 MINUTES
PRESSURE: 2 MINUTES
TOTAL: 30 MINUTES

 SETTINGS: PRESSURE COOK (HIGH)
RELEASE: QUICK

1 Rinse and dry the mushrooms. Remove the mushroom stems and scrape out the gills with a spoon. In a medium bowl, whisk together the balsamic vinegar, tamari, and garlic. Add the mushrooms to the bowl and brush with the marinade. Let sit for 15 minutes.

2 Fit the inner pot with the trivet or steam rack and add 1 cup water. Remove the mushrooms from the marinade and place top-down on the trivet, overlapping slightly if needed.

3 Lock the lid and ensure the steam release valve is set to the sealing position. Select **Pressure Cook (High),** and set the cook time for **2 minutes.**

4 Once the cook time is complete, immediately quick release the pressure and carefully remove the lid. Use tongs to remove the mushrooms from the pot.

5 Assemble each burger by topping the bottom bun with avocado, 1 mushroom, onion, tomato, and lettuce. Spread the top bun with ketchup and mustard. Enjoy immediately.

4 portobello mushrooms
¼ cup balsamic vinegar
2 tbsp tamari or soy sauce
3 cloves garlic, minced
1 cup water

FOR SERVING:
4 vegan hamburger buns, toasted
1 avocado, sliced or mashed
1 small red onion, sliced into rings
1 large tomato, sliced
1 small head romaine lettuce
Ketchup, to taste
Yellow or Dijon mustard, to taste

tip *This recipe is easy to make gluten-free by using plant-based gluten-free buns or swapping the buns for lettuce wraps.*

Nutrition per serving:
CALORIES: 249; **TOTAL FAT:** 9g; **SATURATED FAT:** 1.5g; **CHOLESTEROL:** 0mg; **SODIUM:** 525mg; **TOTAL CARBOHYDRATE:** 35g; **FIBER:** 6g; **PROTEIN:** 8g

SERVES: 4

 PREP: 10 MINUTES
PRESSURE: 5 MINUTES
TOTAL: 30 MINUTES

 SETTINGS: PRESSURE COOK (HIGH),
SAUTÉ (MEDIUM)
RELEASE: NATURAL, QUICK

2 (20oz; 570g) cans jackfruit
in brine or water

1 cup water

½ cup Homemade BBQ Sauce (see
p156), or vegan store-bought BBQ
sauce (gluten-free, if needed), plus
more for serving

FOR THE COLESLAW:

¼ cup vegan mayonnaise
(gluten-free, if needed)

1 tbsp pure maple syrup

2 tbsp apple cider vinegar

Sea salt, to taste

Freshly ground black pepper,
to taste

4 cups shredded cabbage
(about 9oz; 255g bag)

1 medium carrot, shredded

FOR SERVING:

4 vegan buns or multigrain bread,
toasted (gluten-free, if needed)

1 tomato, sliced

Sliced pickles

1 small red onion, thinly sliced

PULLED JACKFRUIT SANDWICHES
with Coleslaw

Sweet, smoky, and savory BBQ jackfruit paired with fresh, crunchy
coleslaw makes a delicious sandwich filling.

1 Drain and rinse the jackfruit in a colander. Cut the jackfruit into
½-inch (1.25cm) pieces going with the direction of the fibers, from
the core outward.

2 Fit the inner pot with a steamer basket, and add 1 cup water. Add
the jackfruit pieces to the steamer basket. Lock the lid and ensure the
steam release valve is set to the sealing position. Select **Pressure Cook
(High),** and set the cook time for **5 minutes.**

3 Once the cook time is complete, allow the pressure to release naturally
for 3 minutes, then quick release any remaining pressure. Carefully
remove the lid. Remove the steamer basket, drain the water, and
return the jackfruit to the inner pot. Select **Sauté (Medium),** and add
the BBQ sauce. Use a potato masher to mash the jackfruit into stringy,
bite-sized pieces.

4 Meanwhile, make the coleslaw. In a medium bowl, whisk together the
mayonnaise, maple syrup, vinegar, and a pinch of salt and pepper to
taste. Toss in the cabbage and carrot to coat.

5 To serve, top the buns with a generous layer of coleslaw and jackfruit.
Top with tomato, pickles, and red onion. Serve immediately with more
BBQ sauce on the side.

tip *For a heartier sandwich with more protein, add 1½ cups cooked
white beans, such as cannellini, after "pulling" the jackfruit. Let the
beans heat up with the BBQ sauce on Sauté mode.*

Nutrition per serving:
CALORIES: 566; **TOTAL FAT:** 15g; **SATURATED FAT:** 2g; **CHOLESTEROL:** 0mg;
SODIUM: 637mg; **TOTAL CARBOHYDRATE:** 108g; **FIBER:** 6g; **PROTEIN:** 9g

LENTIL SLOPPY JOES

 SERVES: 8

 PREP: 5 MINUTES
PRESSURE: 15 MINUTES
TOTAL: 40 MINUTES

 SETTINGS: SAUTÉ (MEDIUM),
PRESSURE COOK (HIGH)
RELEASE: NATURAL

These sloppy joes have all the flavor you remember from childhood, but without the ground beef. Top with your favorite veggies, vegan coleslaw, or the suggested toppings below for an easy family dinner.

1 Pick over the lentils and discard any stones or debris. Rinse and drain the lentils.

2 Select **Sauté (Medium),** and heat the oil, if using, in the inner pot until hot. (Otherwise, you can dry sauté in the hot pot or add a bit of water in the bottom of the pot.) Add the onion and bell pepper and sauté until softened and golden, 3 to 5 minutes. Press **Cancel.**

3 Add the rinsed lentils, tomato sauce, ketchup, mustard, syrup, chili powder, vinegar, Worcestershire sauce, and vegetable broth. Lock the lid and ensure the steam release valve is set to the sealing position. Select **Pressure Cook (High),** and set the cook time for **15 minutes.**

4 Once the cook time is complete, allow the pressure to release naturally for 10 to 15 minutes, then quick release any remaining pressure. Carefully remove the lid.

5 Add the lentil sloppy joe filling to the buns, and top with slices of onion, greens, and avocado, if using. Serve immediately.

tip *Make these sloppy joes gluten-free by using gluten-free buns or your favorite gluten-free sliced bread.*

1lb (450g) dried green or brown lentils

1 tbsp extra virgin olive oil (optional)

1 yellow onion, chopped

1 green bell pepper, deseeded and chopped

1 (15oz; 420g) can tomato sauce

½ cup ketchup

2 tbsp yellow mustard

2 tbsp pure maple syrup

1 tbsp chili powder

2 tbsp apple cider vinegar

1 tbsp vegan Worcestershire sauce (gluten-free, if needed) (see tip on p113)

4 cups vegetable broth

FOR SERVING:

6 vegan buns, lightly toasted

1 small red onion, thinly sliced

2 cups baby greens, such as arugula

1 avocado (optional), sliced

Nutrition per serving:
CALORIES: 455; **TOTAL FAT:** 9g; **SATURATED FAT:** 2g; **CHOLESTEROL:** 0mg; **SODIUM:** 937mg; **TOTAL CARBOHYDRATE:** 75g; **FIBER:** 22g; **PROTEIN:** 22g

SERVES: 6

PREP: 10 MINUTES
PRESSURE: 20 MINUTES
TOTAL: 1 HOUR

SETTINGS: PRESSURE COOK (HIGH), SAUTÉ (HIGH)
RELEASE: NATURAL

1 cup dried chickpeas, rinsed

4 cups water

1 small yellow onion, chopped

4 cloves garlic, roughly chopped

½ cup fresh cilantro leaves

½ cup flat-leaf parsley leaves

2 tbsp fresh lemon juice

1 tsp ground cumin

1 tsp sea salt

¼ tsp freshly ground black pepper

½ tsp baking powder

1–2 tbsp chickpea flour or all-purpose flour

2 tbsp extra virgin olive oil

FOR THE TAHINI SAUCE:

¼ cup tahini

3 tbsp fresh lemon juice

1 clove garlic, minced

½ tsp sea salt

Pinch of freshly ground black pepper

Pinch of ground cumin

4 tbsp water

FOR SERVING:

6 small pita bread rounds

1 plum tomato, sliced

1 small red onion, sliced

2 cups baby spinach

FALAFEL PITAS
with Tahini Sauce

The best falafel are made with soaked chickpeas—not cooked or canned. Here, chickpeas get a quick soak in the Instant Pot rather than waiting 12 hours or more.

1 Add the chickpeas and 4 cups water to the inner pot. Lock the lid and ensure the steam release valve is set to the sealing position. Select **Pressure Cook (High),** and set the cook time for **20 minutes.**

2 Once the cook time is complete, allow the pressure to release naturally. Carefully remove the lid and drain the chickpeas. They will be rehydrated but not completely cooked through.

3 Preheat the oven to 425°F (220°C). Transfer the chickpeas to a food processor and add the onion, garlic, cilantro, parsley, lemon juice, cumin, salt, pepper, and baking powder. Pulse until all ingredients are finely chopped but not puréed. Pulse in the flour to help bind the mixture, adding more flour as needed if the mixture is too damp from the still-wet chickpeas or herbs.

4 Add the oil to the inner pot or a large skillet. Select **Sauté (High),** or heat the pan over medium-high heat. Scoop heaping tablespoon-sized balls of the falafel mixture (a small cookie scoop works well) and flatten into ¾-inch (2cm) thick patties. Fry until well browned on each side, adding more oil as needed.

5 Transfer the browned patties to a baking sheet and bake for 10 minutes.

6 Meanwhile, make the tahini sauce. In a small bowl, whisk together all ingredients, adding up to 4 tablespoons water as needed to thin.

7 Stuff the pita pockets with the falafel, tomato, onion, and spinach. Drizzle with tahini sauce. Serve immediately.

tip *Falafel reheat well in the oven, making this a great meal prep recipe.*

Nutrition per serving:
CALORIES: 319; **TOTAL FAT:** 13g; **SATURATED FAT:** 2g; **CHOLESTEROL:** 0mg; **SODIUM:** 765mg; **TOTAL CARBOHYDRATE:** 43g; **FIBER:** 10g; **PROTEIN:** 12g

SERVES: 4

 PREP: 1 MINUTE
PRESSURE: 12–14 MINUTES
TOTAL: 30 MINUTES

 SETTINGS: PRESSURE COOK (HIGH)
RELEASE: NATURAL

1 cup water

4 medium russet potatoes

SUGGESTIONS FOR SERVING:

1 batch of Baked Beans (see p113)

1 batch of Sweet Potato and
Quinoa Chili (see p78)

1 batch of Simple Cashew Cream
(see p156) with nutritional yeast
and roasted broccoli florets

JACKET POTATOES

Jacket potatoes, popular in the UK and more commonly known as baked potatoes in the US, are soft and fluffy on the inside. They are tasty on their own with a little vegan butter or topped with everything from beans to chili to cashew cream.

1 Fit the inner pot with the trivet or steam rack and add 1 cup water. Prick the potatoes a few times all over with a fork so that steam can escape. Place the potatoes on the trivet.

2 Lock the lid and ensure the steam release valve is set to the sealing position. Select **Pressure Cook (High),** and set the cook time for **12 to 14 minutes.** The cook time varies depending on size and can take up to 20 minutes for very large potatoes.

3 Once the cook time is complete, allow the pressure to release naturally. Carefully remove the lid and make sure the potatoes are tender. If not pressure cook for 3 minutes more.

4 Carefully remove the potatoes and cut open. Top with your desired toppings and serve immediately.

tip *If you'd like to crisp up the skin once they're cooked, brush with olive oil, sprinkle with sea salt, and place into the oven at 450°F (200°C), directly on the top rack, for 5 minutes.*

Nutrition per potato (excluding suggestions for serving):
CALORIES: 149; **TOTAL FAT:** 0g; **SATURATED FAT:** 0g; **CHOLESTEROL:** 0mg;
SODIUM: 38mg; **TOTAL CARBOHYDRATE:** 34g; **FIBER:** 4g; **PROTEIN:** 4g

SHEPHERD-LESS PIE

A warm and cozy comfort food meal, this meat-free version of shepherd's pie is filled with veggies and topped with mashed potatoes.

SERVES: 6

PREP: 10 MINUTES, PLUS MAKING THE MASHED POTATO TOPPING
PRESSURE: 4 MINUTES
TOTAL: 25 MINUTES

SETTINGS: SAUTÉ (MEDIUM), PRESSURE COOK (HIGH)
RELEASE: QUICK

1 Select **Sauté (Medium),** and heat the oil, if using, in the inner pot until hot. (Otherwise, you can dry sauté in the hot pot or add a bit of water in the bottom of the pot.) Add the onion and sauté until softened and golden, 3 to 5 minutes. Add the garlic, carrots, celery, and mushrooms, and sauté 2 minutes more. Add the broth, rosemary, thyme, peas, salt, and pepper, and stir to combine.

2 Lock the lid and ensure the steam release valve is set to the sealing position. Select **Pressure Cook (High),** and set the cook time for **4 minutes.**

3 Once the cook time is complete, immediately quick release the pressure and carefully remove the lid. Remove and discard the thyme stems. Stir in the tomato paste.

4 Preheat the broiler. In a small bowl, whisk together the arrowroot and 1½ tablespoons water. Stir the slurry into the pot to thicken the filling.

5 Transfer the filling mixture to a 9-inch (23cm) pie dish. Spread the mashed potatoes over the filling. Place the dish under the broiler until the potatoes are browned at the peaks. Garnish with parsley, and serve immediately.

1 tsp extra virgin olive oil (optional)

1 small yellow onion, diced

3 cloves garlic, minced

3 carrots, diced

3 stalks celery, diced

8oz (225g) baby bella mushrooms, quartered

1 cup vegetable broth

1 tbsp chopped fresh rosemary

5 sprigs fresh thyme

2 cups frozen peas

1 tsp sea salt

½ tsp freshly ground black pepper

2 tbsp tomato paste

1½ tbsp arrowroot starch or cornstarch

1½ tbsp cool water

1 batch of Truffled Olive Oil Mashed Potatoes (see p109)

¼ cup chopped fresh parsley, for garnish

tip *This is a great recipe to adapt to your own tastes or ingredients you have available. Other foods my family loves in this pie include 1 cup cooked green lentils, roughly chopped green beans, and quartered Brussels sprouts.*

Nutrition per serving:
CALORIES: 290; **TOTAL FAT:** 11g; **SATURATED FAT:** 2g; **CHOLESTEROL:** 0mg; **SODIUM:** 647mg; **TOTAL CARBOHYDRATE:** 44g; **FIBER:** 8g; **PROTEIN:** 8g

VEGGIE POT PIE

It's doesn't get much more comforting than warm veggies in a creamy sauce topped with light and buttery puff pastry.

 SERVES: 4

 PREP: 10 MINUTES
PRESSURE: 3 MINUTES
TOTAL: 45 MINUTES

 SETTINGS: SAUTÉ (MEDIUM),
PRESSURE COOK (HIGH)
RELEASE: NATURAL, QUICK

1 Preheat the oven to 400°F (200°C). Roll out the puff pastry on a sheet of parchment or a silicone baking mat. Turn a 9-inch (23cm) pie dish upside down onto the pastry and use as a template to cut a circle just slightly larger than the top of the pie dish. Discard the scraps. Cut slits in the center for decoration. Place on a baking sheet and transfer to the oven. Bake until golden brown and cooked through, about 10 minutes. Set aside.

2 Select **Sauté (Medium),** and heat the oil, if using, in the inner pot until hot. (Otherwise, you can dry sauté in the hot pot or add a bit of water in the bottom of the pot.) Add the onion and sauté until softened and golden, 3 to 5 minutes. Press **Cancel.** Add the potatoes, carrots, celery, butternut squash, corn, salt, pepper, sage, leaves from half of the thyme, and broth. Stir to combine.

3 Lock the lid and ensure the steam release valve is set to the sealing position. Select **Pressure Cook (High),** and set the cook time for **3 minutes.**

4 Once the cook time is complete, allow the pressure to release naturally for 3 minutes, then quick release any remaining pressure. Carefully remove the lid. Press **Cancel.**

5 Meanwhile, make the roux. In a small saucepan, melt the butter over medium heat. Whisk in the flour. Cook for 3 minutes, stirring occasionally.

6 Select **Sauté (Medium).** Whisk the roux into the vegetable mixture. Whisk in the garlic powder and the leaves from the remaining thyme, reserving a few for garnish. Simmer, stirring, until the mixture has thickened, about 2 minutes. Stir in the peas. Press **Cancel.** Season to taste with salt and pepper.

7 Pour the vegetable pot pie filling into the pie dish. Place the puff pastry crust on top of the filling. Garnish with the remaining thyme leaves. Let cool for 10 minutes, then serve.

1 sheet frozen vegan puff pastry (such as Aussie Bakery), thawed

1 tbsp extra virgin olive oil (optional)

1 yellow onion, diced

1½ cups diced yellow or red potatoes

3 carrots, sliced

3 celery stalks, sliced

1½ cups 1-in (2.5cm) cubes butternut squash

½ cup frozen corn kernels

1 tsp sea salt

½ tsp freshly ground black pepper

1 tsp dried sage

5 sprigs fresh thyme, divided

1½ cups vegetable broth

1 tsp garlic powder

1½ cups frozen peas, thawed

FOR THE ROUX:

4 tbsp vegan butter (such as Miyoko's)

6 tbsp all-purpose flour

tip *For a gluten-free option, use a gluten-free pie crust, following the package instructions, and use gluten-free all-purpose flour for the roux.*

Nutrition per serving:
CALORIES: 430; **TOTAL FAT:** 18g; **SATURATED FAT:** 6g; **CHOLESTEROL:** 0mg; **SODIUM:** 738mg; **TOTAL CARBOHYDRATE:** 59g; **FIBER:** 8g; **PROTEIN:** 9g

SERVES: 4

PREP: 5 MINUTES
PRESSURE: 25 MINUTES
TOTAL: 1 HOUR

SETTINGS: SAUTÉ (MEDIUM),
PRESSURE COOK (HIGH),
WARM (LOW)
RELEASE: NATURAL

2 medium butternut squash

2 tbsp extra virgin olive oil, divided

½ tsp sea salt, plus more to taste

Freshly ground black pepper,
to taste

1 small yellow onion, diced

3 cloves garlic, minced

⅔ cup vegetable broth

⅔ cup wild rice mix (brown
basmati rice and wild rice), rinsed

2 cups packed chopped curly kale

⅛ tsp ground cayenne pepper

1 tsp ground sage

1 tbsp tamari

1½ cups cooked chickpeas,
drained

¼ cup dried cranberries

⅓ cup chopped pecans

1 cup chopped flat-leaf parsley

WILD RICE AND CHICKPEA STUFFED BUTTERNUT SQUASH
with Cranberries and Pecans

Butternut squash halves are roasted in the oven while a savory and sweet filling of wild rice, cranberries, pecans, and kale is made in the Instant Pot. This beautiful dish is perfect for a holiday dinner.

1 Preheat the oven to 425°F (220°C). Cut the squash in half lengthwise and scoop out the seeds. Brush the cut sides of the squash with 1 tablespoon oil, and sprinkle with salt and pepper. Place on a baking sheet, cut-side up, and roast until tender and caramelized, about 50 minutes. Scoop the flesh out to create a well along the center of the squash, leaving about a 1-inch (2.5cm) border in the skin. Chop the removed squash flesh into 1-inch (2.5cm) pieces. Set aside.

2 Meanwhile, select **Sauté (Medium),** and heat the remaining 1 tablespoon oil (optional), in the inner pot until hot. (Otherwise, you can dry sauté in the hot pot or add a bit of water in the bottom of the pot.) Add the onion and sauté until softened and golden, 3 to 5 minutes. Add the garlic and sauté 1 minute more. Add the broth to deglaze the pot, scraping up any bits stuck to the bottom. Add the rice and salt, and stir to combine.

3 Lock the lid and ensure the steam release valve is set to the sealing position. Select **Pressure Cook (High),** and set the cook time for **25 minutes.**

4 Once the cook time is complete, allow the pressure to release naturally. Carefully remove the lid and select **Sauté (Medium).** Stir in the kale until wilted, about 2 minutes. Select **Warm (Low).** Stir in all remaining ingredients, including the reserved squash flesh. Spoon the rice mixture into the squash boats. Serve warm.

tip This dish works well as an entrée with 4 butternut squash boats or 8 side dish servings when halved crosswise after filling.

Nutrition per serving:
CALORIES: 471; **TOTAL FAT:** 16g; **SATURATED FAT:** 2g; **CHOLESTEROL:** 0mg; **SODIUM:** 455mg; **TOTAL CARBOHYDRATE:** 79g; **FIBER:** 13g; **PROTEIN:** 13g

CHANA MASALA

This version of the popular Indian chickpea curry is easier and just as delicious as the authentic take-out dish. This recipe is made with ingredients easily found at most grocery stores.

 SERVES: 6

 PREP: 10 MINUTES, PLUS OVERNIGHT FOR SOAKING
PRESSURE: 30 MINUTES
TOTAL: 1 HOUR

 SETTINGS: SAUTÉ (MEDIUM), PRESSURE COOK (HIGH)
RELEASE: NATURAL

1 Drain and rinse chickpeas. Select **Sauté (Medium),** and heat the oil, if using, in the inner pot until hot. (Otherwise, you can dry sauté in the hot pot or add a bit of water in the bottom of the pot.) Add the onion and sauté until softened and golden, 3 to 5 minutes. Add the garlic, ginger, cumin, garam masala, turmeric, coriander, and bay leaf, and sauté 1 minute more. Select **Cancel.**

2 Add 2¼ cups water to deglaze the pan, scraping up any bits stuck to the bottom of the pot. Add the chickpeas and salt, and stir to combine. There should be just enough water to cover the chickpeas, but add more if needed. Add the tomatoes on top of the chickpeas, but do not stir.

3 Lock the lid and ensure the steam release valve is set to the sealing position. Select **Pressure Cook (High),** and set the cook time for **30 minutes.**

4 Once the cook time is complete, allow the pressure to release naturally. Carefully remove the lid. If desired, stir in the cayenne to taste. Stir in the lemon juice. Serve warm with rice, and garnish generously with fresh cilantro and a dollop of yogurt.

2 cups dried chickpeas, soaked overnight

1 tbsp coconut oil (optional)

1 yellow onion, chopped

4 cloves garlic, minced

1 tbsp freshly grated ginger

1 tbsp cumin seeds

1 tsp garam masala

1 tsp ground turmeric

1 tsp ground coriander

1 bay leaf

2¼ cups water

1 tsp sea salt

2 cups crushed tomatoes

¼ tsp ground cayenne (optional)

Juice of ½ small lemon

FOR SERVING:

1 batch of Basic White Basmati Rice or Basic Long-Grain Brown Rice (see p116)

Fresh cilantro leaves

Dairy-free plain yogurt (optional)

tip *For a nutritious boost, wilt in 5 ounces (140g; about 4 cups) baby spinach at the very end or serve with roasted cauliflower or a green salad.*

Nutrition per serving (excluding foods for serving):
CALORIES: 287; **TOTAL FAT:** 6g; **SATURATED FAT:** 2g; **CHOLESTEROL:** 0mg; **SODIUM:** 437mg; **TOTAL CARBOHYDRATE:** 46g; **FIBER:** 13g; **PROTEIN:** 14g

SERVES: 4

PREP: 5 MINUTES
PRESSURE: 2 MINUTES
TOTAL: 15 MINUTES

SETTINGS: SAUTÉ (MEDIUM), PRESSURE COOK (HIGH)
RELEASE: QUICK

1 tbsp coconut oil or extra virgin olive oil (optional)

1 yellow onion, diced

1 tbsp water

1–3 tbsp yellow curry paste

1 (15fl oz; 445ml) can coconut milk (light or regular)

1 tsp ground turmeric powder

1 tsp coconut sugar

3 cups cooked and drained chickpeas

2 cups (1-in; 2.5cm) sweet potato chunks, skin on

3oz (85g) baby spinach (about 2 cups)

1 batch of Basic White Basmati Rice (see p116), or Perfect Quinoa (see p117), for serving

1 lime, cut into wedges, for serving

Fresh cilantro leaves, for serving

EASY YELLOW CURRY
with Sweet Potato, Chickpeas, and Spinach

This mild yellow curry is a snap to make with store-bought curry paste, which can be found in Asian grocery stores and online. Coconut milk creates a creamy base, while sweet potatoes lend a bit of sweetness.

1 Select **Sauté (Medium),** and heat the oil, if using, in the inner pot until hot. (Otherwise, you can dry sauté in the hot pot or add a bit of water in the bottom of the pot.) Add the onion and sauté until softened and golden, 3 to 5 minutes.

2 Add the curry paste, and sauté 1 minute more. Add 1 tablespoon water to deglaze the pan if there are any bits stuck to the bottom. Add the coconut milk, turmeric, coconut sugar, chickpeas, and sweet potatoes.

3 Lock the lid and ensure the steam release valve is set to the sealing position. Select **Pressure Cook (High),** and set the cook time for **2 minutes.**

4 Once the cook time is complete, immediately quick release the pressure. Carefully remove the lid, and stir in the spinach to wilt.

5 Serve the curry warm on a bed of rice or quinoa with a lime wedge, and garnish generously with cilantro.

tip *For a mild curry, start with 1 tablespoon curry paste. You can always add more to taste.*

Don't cut your sweet potato pieces too small or let them cook too long; they can easily become too soft.

Nutrition per serving (with light coconut milk and excluding rice):
CALORIES: 300; **TOTAL FAT:** 12g; **SATURATED FAT:** 8g; **CHOLESTEROL:** 0mg; **SODIUM:** 283mg; **TOTAL CARBOHYDRATE:** 38g; **FIBER:** 11g; **PROTEIN:** 11g

SERVES: 4

PREP: 3 MINUTES
PRESSURE: 1 MINUTE
TOTAL: 15 MINUTES

SETTINGS: SAUTÉ (MEDIUM),
PRESSURE COOK (HIGH)
RELEASE: QUICK

1 tbsp extra virgin olive oil (optional)

1 small yellow onion, diced

2 cloves garlic, minced

1 tbsp freshly grated ginger

1 tbsp curry powder

1 tsp turmeric

1½ cups dried split red lentils, picked over and rinsed

1 (15fl oz; 440ml) can unsweetened light coconut milk

1 cup water

½ tsp salt, or to taste

2 cups packed arugula or spinach (optional)

Fresh cilantro, for garnish

Basic White Basmati Rice (see p116) (optional), for serving

Steamed mixed veggies (optional), for serving

SIMPLE RED LENTIL DAL

Dal is a classic Indian side dish made with soft red lentils and aromatic spices. Use it as a side for your own Indian-inspired feast or as an easy main dish with vegetables and rice. While not traditional, I love wilting in a couple handfuls of arugula or spinach.

1   Select **Sauté (Medium),** and heat the oil, if using, in the inner pot until hot. (Otherwise, you can dry sauté in the hot pot or add a bit of water in the bottom of the pot.) Add the onion and sauté until softened and golden, 3 to 5 minutes. Press **Cancel.** Add a splash of water and deglaze the pot, scraping up any little pieces of onion that may be stuck to the bottom.

2   Add the garlic, ginger, curry powder, and turmeric, and stir to combine. Add the lentils, coconut milk, and 1 cup water. Lock the lid and ensure the steam release valve is set to the sealing position. Select **Pressure Cook (High),** and set the cook time for **1 minute.**

3   Once the cook time is complete, immediately quick release the pressure. Carefully remove the lid. Season to taste with the salt. Stir in the arugula, if using. Garnish with fresh cilantro. Serve immediately as a side dish or as a main dish with rice and vegetables.

tip   *Red lentils cook much more quickly than green or brown. One minute at pressure may seem too little, but the lentils will be nearly done by the time the pot reaches pressure. Green lentils would need much longer.*

Nutrition per serving:
CALORIES: 370; **TOTAL FAT:** 11g; **SATURATED FAT:** 5g; **CHOLESTEROL:** 0mg; **SODIUM:** 168mg; **TOTAL CARBOHYDRATE:** 47g; **FIBER:** 12g; **PROTEIN:** 20g

MUSHROOM BOURGUIGNON

This French-inspired stew is made from big, chunky vegetables in a rich and flavorful sauce. Serve with pasta, soft polenta, mashed potatoes, or a chunk of crusty bread for sopping up the juices.

 SERVES: 6

 PREP. 10 MINUTES
PRESSURE: 7 MINUTES, PLUS 0 MINUTES
TOTAL: 42 MINUTES

 SETTINGS: SAUTÉ (MEDIUM), PRESSURE COOK (HIGH)
RELEASE: NATURAL, QUICK

1 Select **Sauté (Medium),** and heat the oil, if using, in the inner pot until hot. (Otherwise, you can dry sauté in the hot pot or add a bit of water in the bottom of the pot.) Add the onion and sauté until softened and golden, 3 to 5 minutes. Add the carrots, celery, and garlic, and sauté 1 minute more. Add the wine to deglaze the pot, scraping up any bits stuck to the bottom. Simmer for 2 minutes to cook off some of the alcohol. Press **Cancel.**

2 Add the vegetable broth, bouillon cube, tomato paste, potatoes, mushrooms, thyme, rosemary, bay leaves, salt, and pepper, and stir to combine. Lock the lid and ensure the steam release valve is set to the sealing position. Select **Pressure Cook (High),** and set the cook time for **7 minutes.**

3 Once the cook time is complete, allow the pressure to release naturally for 5 minutes, then quick release any remaining pressure.

4 Carefully remove the lid and stir in the pearl onions. Lock the lid again, and ensure the steam release valve is set to the sealing position. Select **Pressure Cook (High),** and set the cook time for **0 minutes.**

5 Once the cook time is complete, allow the pressure to release naturally for 2 minutes, then quick release any remaining pressure.

6 In a small bowl, whisk together the arrowroot and 2 tablespoons water. Carefully remove the lid and stir in the arrowroot slurry. Select **Sauté (High),** and simmer for 1 minute to thicken slightly. Remove the thyme stems. Serve the stew immediately with cooked pasta, polenta, mashed potatoes, or in a bowl with crusty bread. Garnish with parsley.

1 tsp extra virgin olive oil (optional)

½ yellow onion, diced

2 carrots, peeled and cut diagonally into 1-in (2.5cm) pieces

2 stalks celery, cut into ½-in (1.25cm) slices

4 cloves garlic, minced

1 cup red wine (or broth) (see tip)

2 cups vegetable broth

1 vegan beef-flavored bouillon cube

2 tbsp tomato paste

6 baby yellow potatoes, halved

1lb (450g) baby bella mushrooms, halved

5 sprigs fresh thyme

1 tbsp chopped fresh rosemary

2 bay leaves

1 tsp sea salt

¼ tsp freshly ground black pepper

¾ cup pearl onions, peeled (thawed if using frozen)

1 tbsp arrowroot starch or cornstarch

2 tbsp water

Pasta, polenta, mashed potatoes, or crusty French bread, for serving

½ cup flat-leaf parsley, for garnish

tip *Bourguignon is traditionally made with red wine, which adds rich flavor and color. Less alcohol cooks off in pressure cooking than with traditional methods, so it's best to only use wine when serving adults.*

Nutrition per serving (excluding pasta, polenta, potatoes, or bread):
CALORIES: 159; **TOTAL FAT:** 1g; **SATURATED FAT:** 0g; **CHOLESTEROL:** 0mg; **SODIUM:** 336mg; **TOTAL CARBOHYDRATE:** 28g; **FIBER:** 4g; **PROTEIN:** 5g

KITCHARI

A one-pot dal and rice meal infused with aromatic spices, kitchari is an ancient Indian recipe with many spellings and variations. It's loved in Ayurvedic medicine for its easy digestibility and is thought to have detoxifying properties.

 SERVES: 4

 PREP: 10 MINUTES
PRESSURE: 6 MINUTES
TOTAL: 40 MINUTES

 SETTINGS: SAUTÉ (MEDIUM), PRESSURE COOK (HIGH)
RELEASE: NATURAL, QUICK

1 Select **Sauté (Medium),** and heat the oil, if using, in the inner pot until hot. (Otherwise, you can dry sauté in the hot pot or add a bit of water in the bottom of the pot.) Add the mustard seeds and cumin seeds, and toast for 1 minute. Add the garlic, ginger, cumin, turmeric, and salt, and sauté 1 minute more. Add the dal, rice, and 3 cups broth, and stir to combine.

2 Lock the lid and ensure the steam release valve is in the sealing position. Select **Pressure Cook (High),** and set the cook time for **6 minutes.**

3 Once the cook time is complete, allow the pressure to release naturally for 7 minutes, then quick release any remaining pressure. Carefully remove the lid.

4 Stir in the spinach or kale and remaining 1 cup broth. Place the lid back on for 2 minutes to wilt the kale. Then stir in more broth as needed to thin to desired consistency.

5 Serve immediately, garnished with cilantro, red pepper flakes, and coconut milk yogurt, if using.

1 tbsp coconut oil (optional)

1 tbsp mustard seeds

½ tsp cumin seeds

2 cloves garlic, minced

1 tbsp freshly grated ginger

½ tsp ground cumin

1 tsp ground turmeric

½ tsp sea salt

1 cup dried yellow mung dal, rinsed

½ cup uncooked basmati rice, rinsed

4 cups vegetable broth, divided

3 cups baby spinach or kale, chopped

1 cup fresh cilantro leaves, for garnish

Red pepper flakes (optional), for garnish

6oz (170g) plain coconut milk yogurt (optional), for serving

tip *Kitchari is meant to be made with a variety of vegetables, so feel free to make the recipe your own. Carrots work best with the cook time, but when they're in season, you could also add sautéed zucchini or other veggies just before serving.*

Nutrition per serving (excluding yogurt):
CALORIES: 264; **TOTAL FAT:** 4g; **SATURATED FAT:** 3g; **CHOLESTEROL:** 0mg; **SODIUM:** 717mg; **TOTAL CARBOHYDRATE:** 46g; **FIBER:** 7g; **PROTEIN:** 11g

SERVES: 8

PREP: 10 MINUTES
PRESSURE: 10 MINUTES
TOTAL: 40 MINUTES

SETTINGS: SAUTÉ (MEDIUM), PRESSURE COOK (HIGH)
RELEASE: NATURAL

1 tbsp extra virgin olive oil

½ yellow onion, chopped

1 carrot, diced

1 stalk celery, diced

3 cloves garlic, minced

8oz (225g) tempeh, finely chopped

½ cup red wine (or broth) (see tip on p57)

1 (26oz; 735g) box finely chopped tomatoes

1 tbsp Italian Seasoning Blend (see p155)

1 tsp fennel seeds

1 tsp sea salt

1 tbsp tamari

1 cup water

1 tbsp balsamic vinegar

1 tbsp pure maple syrup (optional)

Freshly ground black pepper, to taste

1 bunch fresh basil or flat-leaf parsley, chopped

TEMPEH BOLOGNESE

This rich and hearty tomato sauce is loaded with veggies and plant-based protein. Tempeh Bolognese is delicious served over pasta, spaghetti squash, zucchini noodles, or polenta.

1 Select **Sauté (Medium),** and heat the oil in the inner pot. Add the onion, carrots, and celery, and sauté until softened, about 5 minutes. Add the garlic and tempeh, and sauté for 3 minutes more. Add the wine to deglaze the pan, scraping up all the browned bits stuck to the bottom of the pot—any pieces stuck may trigger the burn warning.

2 Add the tomatoes, Italian Seasoning Blend, fennel seeds, salt, tamari, and 1 cup water. Stir to combine. Lock the lid and ensure the steam release valve is set to the sealing position. Select **Pressure Cook (High),** and set the cook time for **10 minutes.**

3 Once the cook time is complete, allow the pressure to release naturally. Carefully remove the lid. If you would like thicker sauce, simmer for a few minutes with **Sauté (Medium).**

4 Stir in the balsamic vinegar. Taste and add maple syrup if needed for sweetness and to cut the acidity, and add more salt and pepper to taste. Stir a handful of the fresh herbs into the sauce, and serve the remaining fresh herbs on the side for garnish. Serve immediately over your favorite pasta.

tip *Tempeh comes vacuum-packed and ready to eat, but it can sometimes be slightly bitter. Some of that bitterness can be removed by steaming or simmering for 10 minutes on the stove. I don't find that step necessary in this recipe, but simmering the sauce on Sauté mode for a few minutes after cooking can help if you find it does have any bitterness.*

Nutrition per serving:
CALORIES: 164; **TOTAL FAT:** 7.5g; **SATURATED FAT:** 1g; **CHOLESTEROL:** 0mg; **SODIUM:** 560mg; **TOTAL CARBOHYDRATE:** 14g; **FIBER:** 2g; **PROTEIN:** 10g

RAMEN NOODLE BOWLS

A warming homemade broth infused with ginger and umami flavors is served in bowls loaded up with ramen noodles, tofu, and vegetables. Add any additional veggies you like to your ramen bowls. Sautéed bok choy, asparagus, edamame, and broccoli would all be delicious.

1 To make the broth, add the kombu, garlic, ginger, and 7 cups water to the inner pot. Lock the lid and ensure the steam release valve is set to the sealing position. Select **Pressure Cook (High),** and set the cook time for **5 minutes.**

2 Once the cook time is complete, allow the pressure to release naturally. Carefully remove the lid and select **Sauté (High).** Simmer for 5 minutes to let the broth reduce slightly and concentrate the flavors. Press **Cancel.** Strain the broth through a fine-mesh sieve to remove the kombu and large pieces of garlic and ginger. Discard the solids and pour the broth back into the inner pot. Whisk in the miso paste and soy sauce.

3 Meanwhile, prepare the tofu, vegetables, and noodles. Toss the tofu with the cornstarch to coat. In a large skillet, heat the oil over medium-high heat. Fry the tofu until golden and crisp, turning to crisp all sides. Remove from the skillet and set aside. Then sauté the mushrooms until tender, about 7 minutes.

4 In a separate saucepan, cook the noodles according to the package instructions. (Do not use any seasonings that may have come with the noodles.) Drain.

5 Assemble the bowls by placing the spinach, carrots, and cooked noodles into large soup bowls. Pour the broth over, and garnish with green onion. Serve immediately with Sriracha on the side to add heat to individual bowls, to taste.

 SERVES: 4

 PREP: 5 MINUTES
PRESSURE: 5 MINUTES
TOTAL: 1 HOUR 5 MINUTES

 SETTINGS: PRESSURE COOK (HIGH), SAUTÉ (HIGH)
RELEASE: NATURAL

1 (14oz; 400g) block extra-firm organic tofu, drained and cubed

3 tbsp organic cornstarch

2 tbsp extra virgin olive oil

2 cups sliced mushrooms

6 cups fresh baby spinach

1 carrot, grated or thinly julienned

2 green onions, thinly sliced

Sriracha sauce, for serving

FOR THE BROTH:

2 large pieces kombu

4 cloves garlic, minced

2 tbsp freshly grated ginger

7 cups water

1 tbsp white miso paste

4 tbsp soy sauce (or tamari for gluten-free)

tip *You can find organic ramen noodles at Asian grocery stores and natural foods stores.*

Kombu is a type of seaweed that gives Dashi (a Japanese broth) and this ramen broth its wonderful umami. Found dried in Asian grocery stores, kombu is high in nutrients, especially iodine. You could also add a strip to the pot when cooking beans, as it helps them become more digestible.

Nutrition per serving:
CALORIES: 360; **TOTAL FAT:** 12g; **SATURATED FAT:** 2g; **CHOLESTEROL:** 0mg; **SODIUM:** 1218mg; **TOTAL CARBOHYDRATE:** 42g; **FIBER:** 7g; **PROTEIN:** 19g

CUBAN BLACK BEAN BOWLS
with Mango Salsa

 SERVES: 6

 PREP: 5 MINUTES
PRESSURE: 27 MINUTES
TOTAL: 1 HOUR

 SETTINGS: SAUTÉ (MEDIUM),
PRESSURE COOK (HIGH)
RELEASE: NATURAL, QUICK

FOR THE CUBAN BLACK BEANS:

1 tbsp extra virgin olive oil (optional)

1 yellow onion, diced

3 cloves garlic, minced

1 green bell pepper, deseeded and diced

2 cups dried black beans, rinsed

1 tbsp ground cumin

2 bay leaves

4 cups water

½ tsp sea salt

FOR THE MANGO SALSA:

1 medium mango, peeled and diced

1 shallot, finely diced

Juice of 1 lime

1 clove garlic, minced

¼ cup chopped fresh cilantro

FOR SERVING:

1 batch of Perfect Quinoa (see p117)

3oz (85g) greens (such as arugula or chopped romaine)

1 avocado, sliced

Fresh cilantro

1 lime, cut into wedges

These colorful bowls are filled with hearty, fiber-rich Cuban black beans and quinoa and topped with bright mango salsa, avocado, and greens.

1 Select **Sauté (Medium),** and heat the oil, if using, in the inner pot until hot. (Otherwise, you can dry sauté in the hot pot or add a bit of water in the bottom of the pot.) Add the onion and sauté until softened and golden, 3 to 5 minutes. Add the garlic and bell pepper and sauté 1 minute more.

2 Add the beans, cumin, bay leaves, and 4 cups water. Lock the lid and ensure the steam release valve is set to the sealing position. Select **Pressure Cook (High),** and set the cook time for **27 minutes.**

3 Once the cook time is complete, allow the pressure to release naturally for 15 minutes, then quick release any remaining pressure. Carefully remove the lid and check that the beans are tender. Remove the bay leaves. Season to taste with salt.

4 To make the mango salsa, in a medium bowl, combine all ingredients.

5 To assemble each bowl, place about ⅔ cup quinoa into the bowl and top with beans, salsa, greens, and avocado. Garnish with fresh cilantro and serve with lime wedges.

tip *This recipe makes about 4 cups of Cuban black beans. If you have extra after making the bowls, freeze them for later. They're also great in tacos!*

Nutrition per serving (excluding foods for serving):
CALORIES: 254; **TOTAL FAT:** 3g; **SATURATED FAT:** 0g; **CHOLESTEROL:** 0mg; **SODIUM:** 53mg; **TOTAL CARBOHYDRATE:** 47g; **FIBER:** 15g; **PROTEIN:** 13g

SERVES: 4

 PREP: 5 MINUTES
PRESSURE: 4 MINUTES
TOTAL: 25 MINUTES

 SETTINGS: SAUTÉ (MEDIUM),
PRESSURE COOK (HIGH)
RELEASE: QUICK

1 tbsp extra virgin olive oil

4 vegan Italian sausages
(such as Beyond Meat or Field
Roast) (soy-free and gluten-free,
if needed)

1 yellow onion, halved and sliced

¼ cup dry white wine (such as
Pinot Grigio) (or broth) (see tip
on p57)

¼ cup water

1 red bell pepper, deseeded and
cut into ¼-in (½cm) strips

1 yellow bell pepper, deseeded
and cut into ¼-in (½cm) strips

1 orange bell pepper, deseeded
and cut into ¼-in (½cm) strips

1½ tbsp Italian Seasoning Blend
(see p155)

1 (15oz; 420g) can crushed
tomatoes

1 tsp balsamic vinegar

Sea salt, to taste

Freshly ground black pepper,
to taste

1 cup fresh basil leaves, for garnish

ITALIAN SAUSAGE, PEPPERS, AND ONIONS

This is one of my husband's favorite dinners from his omnivorous days, and it's easy to make free of animal products with plant-based "sausages." It's filled with Italian flavor: fresh and dried herbs, onions, peppers, and a tomato base. Serve as sandwiches inside rolls and alongside spaghetti or atop creamy polenta.

1 Select **Sauté (Medium),** and heat the oil in the inner pot until very hot. Add the sausages and brown on all sides, turning occasionally with tongs. When the sausages are completely cooked through according to the package instructions, remove and set on a plate. To keep warm, tent with foil or place in the oven heated to 200°F (95°C).

2 Add the sliced onion to the inner pot. Sauté until softened and golden, 3 to 5 minutes. Add the wine to deglaze the pan, scraping up any browned bits stuck to the bottom. Press **Cancel.**

3 Without stirring, add ¼ cup water, bell peppers, Italian Seasoning Blend, and tomatoes, layering in that order. Lock the lid and ensure the steam release valve is set to the sealing position. Select **Pressure Cook (High),** and set the cook time for **4 minutes.**

4 Once the cook time is complete, immediately quick release the pressure and carefully remove the lid. If the peppers aren't soft enough yet, turn the pot to **Sauté (High),** and cook until softened. If you'd like to thicken up the sauce, simmer for a couple of minutes more.

5 Stir in the balsamic vinegar and season to taste with salt and pepper. Serve the peppers and onions immediately, topped with the sausages. Garnish with fresh basil.

tip *Either hot or sweet Italian sausages work well here—whichever you prefer!*

Nutrition per serving:
CALORIES: 322; **TOTAL FAT:** 12g; **SATURATED FAT:** 1g; **CHOLESTEROL:** 0mg;
SODIUM: 802mg; **TOTAL CARBOHYDRATE:** 28g; **FIBER:** 4g; **PROTEIN:** 28g

BUTTERNUT SQUASH MAC AND CHEEZE

Coated in a creamy, savory butternut squash sauce and topped with crunchy, buttery bread crumbs, this dreamy mac and "cheese" is a tasty family main dish.

 SERVES: 8

 PREP: 10 MINUTES
PRESSURE: 6 MINUTES
TOTAL: 45 MINUTES

 SETTINGS: PRESSURE COOK (HIGH)
RELEASE: NATURAL, QUICK

1 In the inner pot, stir to combine the cashews, squash, salt, and broth. Lock the lid and ensure the steam release valve is set to the sealing position. Select **Pressure Cook (High),** and set the cook time for **6 minutes.**

2 Meanwhile, cook the pasta on the stove according to the package instructions. Drain when the pasta is al dente and place in a 9 x 13-inch (23 x 33cm) casserole dish.

3 Once the pressure cook time is complete, allow the pressure to release naturally for 12 minutes, then quick release any remaining pressure. Carefully remove the lid and make sure the squash is very tender. If not yet tender, pressure cook for 2 minutes more.

4 Carefully transfer the cashew and squash mixture to a blender, working in batches as needed. Add the onion, nutritional yeast, garlic powder, mustard, paprika, and a pinch of pepper. Place the lid on the blender with the center hole open to allow steam to escape. Cover with a towel, and blend until very smooth and creamy. You may need to use a tamper to get the mixture moving at first. Turn off the blender and add more salt and pepper to taste.

5 Pour the sauce over the pasta in the casserole dish, and toss to coat. Preheat the broiler.

6 To make the panko topping, in a small bowl, stir together the panko and melted butter. Season with salt and pepper. Sprinkle over the pasta. Transfer the casserole dish to the oven, and broil until the topping is golden brown, 2 to 3 minutes, watching closely to prevent burning. Serve immediately.

½ cup raw cashews

5 cups 1-in (2.5cm) cubed butternut squash (about 1 small squash)

1 tsp sea salt

1 cup vegetable broth

1lb (450g) uncooked pasta, such as elbow, penne, or cavatappi

1 small yellow onion, roughly chopped

½ cup nutritional yeast (such as Bragg or Trader Joe's)

1 tsp garlic powder

1½ tsp dry mustard

¼ tsp paprika

Freshly ground black pepper

FOR THE PANKO TOPPING:

1 cup panko bread crumbs

3 tbsp melted vegan butter

Sea salt, to taste

Freshly ground black pepper, to taste

tip *This recipe is easy to make gluten-free. Simply use gluten-free pasta and bread crumbs.*

Nutrition per serving:
CALORIES: 363; **TOTAL FAT:** 9g; **SATURATED FAT:** 2g; **CHOLESTEROL:** 0mg; **SODIUM:** 514mg; **TOTAL CARBOHYDRATE:** 46g; **FIBER:** 5g; **PROTEIN:** 12g

VEGETABLE LASAGNA

This incredible lasagna is packed with flavor from the homemade, creamy, dairy-free ricotta and the nutritious veggies. No one can tell this comfort-food classic is vegan—it tastes just like the original, but better!

 SERVES: 6

 PREP: 20 MINUTES
PRESSURE: 24 MINUTES
TOTAL: 1 HOUR 20 MINUTES

 SETTINGS: PRESSURE COOK (HIGH)
RELEASE: NATURAL, QUICK

---

3 cups homemade or store-bought marinara sauce

1 package no-boil lasagna noodles

1 batch Almond Ricotta (see p155)

3 cups baby spinach

1 zucchini, cut crosswise into thin rounds

1 (12oz; 340g) jar roasted red peppers, drained, patted dry, and sliced

1 cup water

¼ cup shredded vegan Parmesan cheese (such as Follow Your Heart) (optional)

1 cup fresh basil, for garnish

---

1 Coat the bottom of a 7-inch (17.5cm) springform pan with a thin layer of marinara sauce. Cover the sauce with lasagna noodle pieces, breaking as needed to fit them in like a puzzle. Spread ⅓ of the ricotta over the noodles with the back of a spoon. Top the ricotta with a layer of spinach leaves, a layer of zucchini rounds, and a layer of red pepper slices. Top the veggies with a layer of sauce. Top the sauce with another layer of broken noodles, ricotta, and veggies continuing in this pattern until there are 3 layers of ricotta and veggies and ending with a fourth layer of noodles. Cover the top layer of noodles with a final layer of sauce.

2 Fit the inner pot with the trivet or steam rack, and add 1 cup water. Cover the springform pan with foil. Place the pan on the trivet. Lock the lid and ensure the steam release valve is set to the sealing position. Select **Pressure Cook (High),** and set the cook time for **24 minutes.**

3 Once the cook time is complete, allow the pressure to release naturally for 10 minutes, then quick release any remaining pressure. Carefully remove the lid and lift the pan out of the pot. Remove the foil. Top the lasagna with Parmesan, if using, and place under the broiler for 5 minutes, or until melted.

4 Let the lasagna rest for 15 minutes before removing the sides of the pan. Garnish with fresh basil, then serve in pie-shaped slices.

Nutrition per serving:
CALORIES: 506; **TOTAL FAT:** 28g; **SATURATED FAT:** 3g; **CHOLESTEROL:** 0mg; **SODIUM:** 787mg; **TOTAL CARBOHYDRATE:** 54g; **FIBER:** 7g; **PROTEIN:** 16g

SERVES: 4

PREP: 5 MINUTES, PLUS OVERNIGHT FOR SOAKING
PRESSURE: 1 MINUTE
TOTAL: 15 MINUTES

SETTINGS: STEAM (HIGH)
RELEASE: QUICK

1 cup water

1 (17oz; 480g) package gluten-free gnocchi

6oz (170g) broccoli florets (about 2 cups)

¼ cup chopped flat-leaf parsley, for garnish

FOR THE ALFREDO SAUCE:

1 cup raw cashews, soaked overnight (see tip)

2 cloves garlic

1 tbsp fresh lemon juice

2 tbsp nutritional yeast (such as Bragg or Trader Joe's)

½ tsp dried rosemary

1 tsp sea salt

Pinch of freshly ground black pepper

Pinch of nutmeg

1 cup water

BROCCOLI ALFREDO GNOCCHI

This ultra creamy and flavorful gnocchi makes an easy and delicious one-pot weeknight meal that's ready in under 30 minutes.

1 To make the alfredo sauce, drain the soaked cashews and add to a blender. Add the garlic, lemon juice, nutritional yeast, rosemary, salt, pepper, and nutmeg. Add ½ cup water. Blend, adding the remaining ½ cup water through the hole in the lid as needed until smooth and creamy.

2 Meanwhile, steam the gnocchi and broccoli. Fit the inner pot with a steamer basket, and add 1 cup water. Add the gnocchi and broccoli to the basket. Lock the lid and ensure the steam release valve is set to the sealing position. Select **Steam (High),** and set the cook time for **1 minute.**

3 Once the cook time is complete, immediately quick release the pressure. Select **Warm.** Carefully remove the lid and the steamer basket. Drain the water from the inner pot. Return the inner pot to the Instant Pot.

4 Add half of the alfredo sauce to the inner pot, and top with the steamed gnocchi and broccoli. Add more sauce to taste—I use about ¾ of the sauce and save the remainder for another use. Stir to coat, adding water to thin to the desired consistency. Serve immediately garnished with fresh parsley.

tip *Raw cashews need to be soft and hydrated before blending. Soak overnight or for at least 6 hours at room temperature, or for at least 2 hours with hot water poured over. It's also important to use raw cashews rather than roasted to avoid a nutty flavor.*

Nutrition per serving:
CALORIES: 413; **TOTAL FAT:** 13g; **SATURATED FAT:** 3g; **CHOLESTEROL:** 21mg; **SODIUM:** 841mg; **TOTAL CARBOHYDRATE:** 63g; **FIBER:** 5g; **PROTEIN:** 13g

ONE POT PASTA
with Cherry Tomatoes and Basil

This simple one-pot pasta is filled with juicy, sweet cherry tomatoes, fresh basil, and salty capers.

SERVES: 6

PREP: 2 MINUTES
PRESSURE: 5 MINUTES
TOTAL: 20 MINUTES

SETTINGS: SAUTÉ (MEDIUM), PRESSURE COOK (LOW)
RELEASE: QUICK

1 tbsp extra virgin olive oil (optional), plus more to serve

1 small yellow onion, diced

4 cloves garlic, sliced

¼ tsp red pepper flakes

1lb (450g) uncooked short pasta (such as penne, fusilli, or bowtie)

1 tsp sea salt

Water, to cover

1pt (551ml) cherry tomatoes

1 bunch fresh basil, torn or sliced

¼ cup drained capers

1 cup shredded vegan Parmesan cheese (such as Follow Your Heart)

Freshly ground black pepper, to taste

1 Select **Sauté (Medium),** and heat the oil, if using, in the inner pot until hot. (Otherwise, you can dry sauté in the hot pot or add a bit of water in the bottom of the pot.) Add the onion and sauté until softened and golden, 3 to 5 minutes. Add the garlic and pepper and sauté 1 minute more. Press **Cancel.**

2 Add the pasta to the inner pot. Add the salt and water until just covered, no more than ¼ inch (0.5cm) above the pasta. Add the tomatoes on top without stirring.

3 Lock the lid and ensure the steam release valve is set to the sealing position. Select **Pressure Cook (Low),** and set the cook time for half of the cook time on the pasta package, rounding down. For example, if the pasta package calls for 10 to 12 minutes on the stove, set the cook time for 5 minutes.

4 Once the cook time is complete, immediately quick release the pressure and carefully remove the lid. Add the fresh basil and capers, and stir to combine. Drizzle with a little olive oil, if desired. Serve immediately with Parmesan and salt and pepper, to taste.

tip *If you're craving more protein, you can stir in a cup of cooked chickpeas or cannellini beans and top with a dollop of Almond Ricotta (see p155), or serve with grilled vegan Italian sausage. If you love greens, wilt in a few handfuls of arugula or spinach at the end.*

Nutrition per serving:
CALORIES: 327; **TOTAL FAT:** 4g; **SATURATED FAT:** 0.5g; **CHOLESTEROL:** 0mg; **SODIUM:** 491mg; **TOTAL CARBOHYDRATE:** 62g; **FIBER:** 4g; **PROTEIN:** 11g

SERVES: 4

 PREP: 10 MINUTES
PRESSURE: 5 MINUTES
TOTAL: 35 MINUTES

 SETTINGS: SAUTÉ (MEDIUM),
PRESSURE COOK (HIGH)
RELEASE: QUICK

FOR THE ROASTED VEGETABLES:

1 small butternut squash, peeled and cut into ½-in (1.25cm) cubes

8–10oz (225–285g) baby Bella mushrooms, cleaned and halved

1lb (450g) Brussels sprouts, halved

3 tbsp avocado oil or extra virgin olive oil

Sea salt, to taste

Freshly ground black pepper, to taste

FOR THE RISOTTO:

1 tbsp extra virgin olive oil (optional)

1 yellow onion, diced

3 cloves garlic, minced

1½ cups dry Arborio rice

4 cups vegetable broth, plus more as needed to thin

3 sprigs fresh thyme, plus more for garnish

½ cup shredded vegan Parmesan cheese (such as Follow Your Heart)

Salt, to taste (recommended truffle salt)

Freshly ground black pepper, to taste

2 cups microgreens or arugula

½ cup pomegranate arils (optional), for garnish

RISOTTO
with Roasted Vegetables

Creamy risotto topped with colorful roasted vegetables makes a comforting and beautiful dinner that's easy enough for busy weeknights but elegant enough for special occasions.

1 To roast the vegetables, preheat the oven to 425°F (220°C). Line a large rimmed baking sheet with parchment paper. Place the squash, mushrooms, and Brussels sprouts on the sheet, and drizzle with the oil. Toss to coat evenly. Season with salt and pepper. Transfer to the oven and roast the vegetables until tender and browned, about 25 minutes. The butternut squash may take longer than the other vegetables to cook; remove the tender veggies and return the squash to the oven until tender and browned, about 10 minutes more.

2 Meanwhile, make the risotto. Select **Sauté (Medium),** and heat the oil, if using, in the inner pot until hot. (Otherwise, you can dry sauté in the hot pot or add a bit of water in the bottom of the pot.) Add the onion and sauté until softened and golden, 3 to 5 minutes. Add the garlic and sauté 1 minute more. Add the rice and toast 1 to 2 minutes.

3 Add the broth and thyme. Lock the lid and ensure the steam release valve is set to the sealing position. Select **Pressure Cook (High),** and set the cook time for **5 minutes.**

4 Once the cook time is complete, immediately quick release the pressure and carefully remove the lid. Stir in the Parmesan and season to taste with salt and pepper. If the risotto is too thick, stir in more broth to thin.

5 Serve the risotto on a bed of greens, topped with the roasted vegetables. Garnish with thyme and pomegranate arils, if using.

tip *Feel free to use whatever veggies you have on hand or are in season. While Brussels sprouts and squash are wonderful during colder months; carrots, zucchini, peas, and artichokes are nice in warmer months. Just remember—veggies don't all cook in the same amount of time, so you may need to adjust.*

Nutrition per serving:
CALORIES: 434; **TOTAL FAT:** 18g; **SATURATED FAT:** 4g; **CHOLESTEROL:** 0mg; **SODIUM:** 873mg; **TOTAL CARBOHYDRATE:** 63g; **FIBER:** 8g; **PROTEIN:** 10g

BUTTERNUT SQUASH SOUP

Creamy and comforting, butternut squash soup has just enough sweetness and a tiny kick of spice, with earthy undertones like sage and nutmeg. This soup is easy enough for a busy weeknight but beautiful enough for your holiday table.

SERVES: 6

PREP: 5 MINUTES
PRESSURE: 6 MINUTES
TOTAL: 35 MINUTES

SETTINGS: SAUTÉ (MEDIUM), PRESSURE COOK (HIGH)
RELEASE: NATURAL, QUICK

1 tbsp extra virgin olive oil (optional)

1 yellow onion, chopped

4 cloves garlic, minced

1 medium butternut squash, peeled and cubed (about 6 cups)

1 carrot, roughly chopped

1 sweet apple (such as Fuji or Gala) peeled, cored, and roughly chopped

7 fresh sage leaves

1½ cups vegetable broth

1 cup canned, unsweetened coconut milk

1 tsp sea salt, plus more to taste

½ tsp ground nutmeg

Pinch of cayenne pepper

OPTIONAL TOPPINGS:

½ cup dairy-free plain yogurt

¼ cup toasted pepitas

½ cup microgreens

3 tbsp pomegranate arils

1   Select **Sauté (Medium),** and heat the oil, if using, in the inner pot until hot. (Otherwise, you can dry sauté in the hot pot or add a bit of water in the bottom of the pot.) Add the onion and sauté until softened and golden, 3 to 5 minutes. Add the garlic and sauté 1 minute more.

2   Add the butternut squash, carrot, apple, sage, broth, coconut milk, salt, nutmeg, and cayenne pepper. Lock the lid and ensure the steam release valve is set to the sealing position. Select **Pressure Cook (High),** and set the cook time for **6 minutes.**

3   Once the cook time is complete, allow the pressure to release naturally for 10 minutes, then quick release any remaining pressure. Press **Cancel.** Carefully remove the lid.

4   Use an immersion blender to blend the soup. Season to taste with nutmeg, additional salt, and more cayenne for heat. For a thicker soup, simmer on Sauté (Medium) for a few minutes.

5   Serve warm, garnished with plain yogurt (or more coconut milk), pepitas, microgreens, and a few pomegranate arils.

tip   *If you're short on time, feel free to use precut butternut squash. You'll need 24 ounces (680g).*

Nutrition per serving (excluding optional toppings):
CALORIES: 212; **TOTAL FAT:** 12g; **SATURATED FAT:** 7.5g; **CHOLESTEROL:** 0mg; **SODIUM:** 390mg; **TOTAL CARBOHYDRATE:** 28g; **FIBER:** 5g; **PROTEIN:** 4g

CURRIED PUMPKIN RED LENTIL SOUP

Subtle pumpkin and coconut flavors spiced up with curry powder create a warming soup for autumn. Red lentils offer fiber to make it more filling.

1 Select **Sauté (High),** and heat the oil, if using, in the inner pot until hot. (Otherwise, you can dry sauté in the hot pot or add a bit of water in the bottom of the pot.) Add the onion and sauté until softened and golden, 3 to 5 minutes. Add the apple, broth, pumpkin, curry powder, cinnamon, nutmeg, lentils, and coconut milk. Stir to combine.

2 Lock the lid and ensure the steam release valve is set to the sealing position. Select **Pressure Cook (High),** and set the cook time for **5 minutes.**

3 Once the cook time is complete, allow the pressure to release naturally for 5 minutes, then quick release any remaining pressure. Carefully remove the lid and stir the soup. Season to taste with additional curry powder, salt, and pepper. Serve immediately topped with cilantro, pepitas, a squeeze of lime juice, and yogurt.

 SERVES: 8

 PREP: 5 MINUTES
PRESSURE: 5 MINUTES
TOTAL: 35 MINUTES

 SETTINGS: SAUTÉ (HIGH), PRESSURE COOK (HIGH)
RELEASE: NATURAL, QUICK

1 tsp coconut oil (optional)

1 small yellow onion, chopped

1 small apple, finely diced

4 cups vegetable broth

1 (15oz; 420g) can pumpkin purée

1 tbsp curry powder, plus more to taste

¼ tsp ground cinnamon

¼ tsp nutmeg

1½ cups dry red lentils, rinsed

1 (15oz; 420g) can unsweetened light coconut milk

Sea salt, to taste

Freshly ground black pepper, to taste

1 small bunch fresh cilantro, for garnish

¼ cup pepitas, for garnish

1 lime, cut into wedges

Dairy-free plain yogurt or cashew cream (optional), for garnish

tip *This soup will thicken as it cools, but if you'd like it thicker right away, select **Sauté (Medium)** after the pressure cooking is complete and simmer for 3 to 5 minutes.*

Nutrition per serving:
CALORIES: 235; **TOTAL FAT:** 7g; **SATURATED FAT:** 3g; **CHOLESTEROL:** 0mg; **SODIUM:** 340mg; **TOTAL CARBOHYDRATE:** 31g; **FIBER:** 8g; **PROTEIN:** 12g

PEANUT TOFU BOWLS

Creamy coconut peanut sauce and tofu are cooked along with rice using the pot-in-pot method. These colorful bowls are loaded up with fresh, raw vegetables, peanuts, sesame seeds, and cilantro for a satisfying and nourishing meal.

1. Drain the tofu and press with paper towels to remove some of the water. Cut into 1-inch (2.5cm) cubes. Select **Sauté (Medium),** and heat the coconut oil until hot. Add the tofu and brown on all sides, turning occasionally.

2. Add the garlic and ginger, and sauté for 1 minute, taking care not to let it burn. Add 1 tablespoon water to deglaze the pan, scraping up any browned bits stuck to the bottom. Add the coconut milk, maple syrup, tamari, and Sriracha sauce.

3. Place the trivet in the inner pot over the tofu mixture. In an oven-safe bowl or baking dish, add the rice, remaining 1 cup water, and salt. Stir to combine, and place the bowl on the trivet.

4. Lock the lid and ensure the steam release valve is set to the sealing position. Select **Pressure Cook (High),** and set the cook time for **3 minutes.**

5. Once the cook time is complete, allow the pressure to release naturally for 15 minutes, then quick release any remaining pressure. Using potholders, carefully remove the lid, the dish of rice, and the trivet. Stir the peanut butter into the tofu mixture. To thicken the sauce, you can simmer on **Sauté** mode for 2 minutes, stirring often. Season the sauce to taste with more Sriracha, syrup, tamari, or peanut butter.

6. Spoon the rice into bowls and top with the peanut sauce and tofu. Arrange the rest of the toppings in the bowls and enjoy immediately.

tip *The peanut butter must be stirred in after pressure cooking so that it does not burn on the bottom.*

SERVES: 4

PREP: 10 MINUTES
PRESSURE: 3 MINUTES
TOTAL: 35 MINUTES

SETTINGS: SAUTÉ (MEDIUM), PRESSURE COOK (HIGH)
RELEASE: NATURAL, QUICK

14oz (400g) extra-firm tofu

1 tbsp coconut oil

3 cloves garlic, minced

1 tbsp freshly minced ginger

1 cup plus 1 tbsp water, divided

1 (13fl oz; 385ml) can coconut milk

1 tbsp pure maple syrup, plus more for serving

3 tbsp tamari, plus more for serving

½ tsp Sriracha sauce, plus more for serving

1 cup long-grain white rice, rinsed and drained

Pinch of sea salt

½ cup peanut butter, plus more for serving

FOR TOPPING:

2 Persian cucumbers, sliced

1 avocado, sliced

2 cups shredded purple cabbage

1 cup shredded carrots, or ribbons

1½oz (40g) microgreens (about 1 cup)

Small bunch fresh cilantro

½ cup peanuts

¼ cup toasted sesame seeds

1 lime, cut into wedges

Nutrition per serving:
CALORIES: 764; **TOTAL FAT:** 47g; **SATURATED FAT:** 23g; **CHOLESTEROL:** 0mg; **SODIUM:** 935mg; **TOTAL CARBOHYDRATE:** 63g; **FIBER:** 10g; **PROTEIN:** 23g

SERVES: 6

PREP: 10 MINUTES, PLUS OVERNIGHT FOR SOAKING
PRESSURE: 6 MINUTES
TOTAL: 35 MINUTES

SETTINGS: SAUTÉ (MEDIUM), PRESSURE COOK (HIGH)
RELEASE: NATURAL, QUICK

1 tbsp extra virgin olive oil (optional)

1 yellow onion, chopped

4 cloves garlic, minced

2 carrots, diced

2 stalks celery, diced

3 cups vegetable broth

1 tbsp chopped fresh oregano

1 tsp sea salt

1½ cups fresh or canned chopped tomatoes with their juices

1½ cups dry black-eyed peas, soaked overnight or quick soaked (see tip)

⅛ cup fresh lemon juice

3 cups chopped, de-stemmed kale leaves

Freshly ground black pepper, to taste

LEMONY IKARIAN LONGEVITY STEW

Coined a Blue Zone by Dan Buettner, the Greek island of Ikaria has one of the highest populations of centenarians in the world and has been referred to as "The Island Where People Forget to Die." Some staples there include wild greens, herbs, homegrown vegetables, lentils, black-eyed peas, herbs, olive oil, and red wine. This soup includes many of those ingredients and is very tasty, too!

1 Select **Sauté (Medium),** and heat the oil, if using, in the inner pot until hot. (Otherwise, you can dry sauté in the hot pot or add a bit of water in the bottom of the pot.) Add the onion and sauté until softened and golden, 3 to 5 minutes. Add the garlic, carrots, and celery, and sauté 1 minute more.

2 Add the broth to deglaze the pan, scraping up any bits that may be stuck to the bottom of the pot. Add the oregano, salt, tomatoes, and soaked black-eyed peas, and stir to combine.

3 Lock the lid and ensure the steam release valve is set to the sealing position. Select **Pressure Cook (High),** and set the cook time for **6 minutes.**

4 Once the cook time is complete, allow the pressure to release naturally for 5 minutes, then quick release any remaining pressure. Carefully remove the lid. Stir in the lemon juice and kale until the kale is wilted. Season to taste with pepper. Serve immediately.

tip To quick-soak the black-eyed peas, bring a pot of water on the stove to a boil, or use the Instant Pot on **Sauté (High).** Add the black-eyed peas, turn off the heat, and cover. Soak for 2 hours before draining.

Nutrition per serving:
CALORIES: 202; **TOTAL FAT:** 3g; **SATURATED FAT:** 0g; **CHOLESTEROL:** 0mg; **SODIUM:** 502mg; **TOTAL CARBOHYDRATE:** 37g; **FIBER:** 8g; **PROTEIN:** 10g

ETHIOPIAN CABBAGE STEW

This comforting Ethiopian-inspired vegetable stew with aromatic spices is quick, easy, and inexpensive. Serve alone, or alongside Ethiopian red lentils and injera (Ethiopian bread) for an unforgettable meal.

SERVES: 4

PREP: 5 MINUTES
PRESSURE: 3 MINUTES
TOTAL: 20 MINUTES

SETTINGS: SAUTÉ (MEDIUM), PRESSURE COOK (HIGH)
RELEASE: QUICK

1   Select **Sauté (Medium),** and heat the oil, if using, in the inner pot until hot. (Otherwise, you can dry sauté in the hot pot or add a bit of water in the bottom of the pot.) Add the onion and sauté until softened and golden, 3 to 5 minutes. Add the ginger, turmeric, and fenugreek, and sauté 1 minute more. Add the vegetable broth to deglaze the pan, scraping up any bits that may be stuck to the bottom. Add the carrots, potatoes, cabbage, salt, and pepper.

2   Lock the lid and ensure the steam release valve is set to the sealing position. Select **Pressure Cook (High),** and set the cook time for **3 minutes.**

3   Once the cook time is complete, immediately quick release the pressure. Carefully remove the lid and make sure the vegetables are tender. If not, lock the lid and pressure cook for 1 minute more.

4   Stir and adjust any seasonings to taste. Serve immediately.

2 tbsp extra virgin olive oil (optional)

1 small yellow onion, sliced

1 tsp freshly grated ginger

½ tsp ground turmeric

¼ tsp fenugreek seeds

⅓ cup vegetable broth

3 large carrots, cut into ¾-in (2cm) slices (about 2 cups)

1lb (450g) gold potatoes, diced into 1-in (2.5cm) cubes (2–3 cups)

½ head cabbage, shredded

1 tsp sea salt

½ tsp freshly ground black pepper

tip *For added protein, add 1½ cups cooked chickpeas or frozen green peas. Fenugreek can be hard to find, but is available at most Indian markets.*

Nutrition per serving:
CALORIES: 209; **TOTAL FAT:** 7g; **SATURATED FAT:** 1g; **CHOLESTEROL:** 0mg;
SODIUM: 391mg; **TOTAL CARBOHYDRATE:** 34g; **FIBER:** 7g; **PROTEIN:** 5g

SERVES: 6

PREP: 10 MINUTES
PRESSURE: 5 MINUTES
TOTAL: 35 MINUTES

SETTINGS: SAUTÉ (MEDIUM),
PRESSURE COOK (HIGH)
RELEASE: QUICK

1 tbsp extra virgin olive oil (optional)

1 large yellow onion, diced

3 cloves garlic, minced

1 green bell pepper, deseeded and diced

1 cup (1-in; 2.5cm) peeled and diced sweet potato cubes

1 (15oz; 420g) can black beans, drained and rinsed

1 (15oz; 420g) can kidney beans, drained and rinsed

1 (4oz; 110g) can diced green chiles

1½ tbsp chili powder

1 tbsp ground cumin

½ tsp smoked paprika

½ tsp sea salt

1 (26oz; 735g) box chopped or diced tomatoes

½ cup uncooked quinoa, rinsed and drained

2 cups vegetable broth

Fresh cilantro leaves, for garnish

1 avocado, sliced, for garnish

SWEET POTATO AND QUINOA CHILI

Hearty, warm, and comforting, this flavorful chili is packed with quinoa, sweet potato, and two types of beans. It's a favorite dinner in my family and is sure to be one in yours, too.

1 Select **Sauté (Medium),** and heat the oil, if using, in the inner pot until hot. (Otherwise, you can dry sauté in the hot pot or add a bit of water in the bottom of the pot.) Add the onion and sauté for 1 minute. Add the garlic, bell pepper, and sweet potatoes, and sauté 1 minute more. Select **Cancel.**

2 Add the black beans, kidney beans, chiles, chili powder, cumin, paprika, salt, tomatoes, quinoa, and broth, and stir. Lock the lid and ensure the steam release valve is set to the sealing position. Select **Pressure Cook (High),** and set the cook time for **5 minutes.**

3 Once the cook time is complete, immediately quick release the pressure and carefully remove the lid. Taste and add more salt or chili powder, if desired. Serve warm, garnished with cilantro and avocado.

tip *This chili is great for meal prep and freezes beautifully. It's also a great option to bring to a friend in need.*

Nutrition per serving:
CALORIES: 295; **TOTAL FAT:** 8g; **SATURATED FAT:** 1g; **CHOLESTEROL:** 0mg; **SODIUM:** 537mg; **TOTAL CARBOHYDRATE:** 48g; **FIBER:** 13g; **PROTEIN:** 12g

SERVES: 6

PREP: 10 MINUTES
PRESSURE: 2 MINUTES
TOTAL: 40 MINUTES

SETTINGS: PRESSURE COOK (HIGH)
RELEASE: NATURAL, QUICK

1 yellow onion, roughly chopped

5 cloves garlic

1 red bell pepper, deseeded and roughly chopped

8 cups Roma tomatoes, halved and deseeded

1 tbsp extra virgin olive oil

1 tsp sea salt, plus more to taste

Freshly ground black pepper, to taste

2 cups vegetable broth

1 cup loosely packed fresh basil leaves, plus more to garnish

TOMATO BASIL SOUP

The tastiest tomato soup is made with fresh, ripe tomatoes roasted with onions and garlic. Bell pepper adds depth of flavor and creaminess, while basil adds bright freshness. Serve this simple soup with avocado toast or a vegan grilled cheese for a comforting family dinner.

1 Preheat the oven to 450°F (230°C). Line a large baking sheet with parchment paper. Place the onion, garlic, bell pepper, and tomato halves on the parchment. Drizzle with olive oil and season with salt and pepper. Roast for about 20 minutes, or until all the ingredients are caramelized. Occasionally check and turn any pieces that are turning too brown.

2 Add the broth and roasted vegetables to the inner pot. Lock the lid and ensure the steam release valve is set to the sealing position. Select **Pressure Cook (High),** and set the cook time for **2 minutes.**

3 Once the cook time is complete, allow the pressure to release naturally for 5 minutes, then quick release any remaining pressure.

4 Carefully remove the lid and transfer the tomato mixture and basil to a blender, working in batches as needed. Place the lid on the blender with the center hole open to allow steam to escape. Cover with a towel. Carefully and slowly blend the tomato mixture until smooth.

5 Pour the mixture back into the inner pot and set to **Warm** until ready to serve. Season with more salt and pepper to taste, and garnish with more fresh basil.

tip *Taking the extra time to roast the onions, garlic, tomatoes, and peppers creates the best flavor. If you're in a hurry, you can brown the veggies in olive oil in the inner pot on* **Sauté (Medium).**

Nutrition per serving:
CALORIES: 60; **TOTAL FAT:** 3g; **SATURATED FAT:** 0g; **CHOLESTEROL:** 0mg
SODIUM: 448mg; **TOTAL CARBOHYDRATE:** 9g; **FIBER:** 1g; **PROTEIN:** 1g

SPLIT PEA SOUP

Split pea soup is a very easy, creamy, cozy, and nourishing meal. Serve with garlic bread, a vegan grilled cheese, or a side salad.

 SERVES: 4

 PREP: 5 MINUTES
PRESSURE: 15 MINUTES
TOTAL: 40 MINUTES

 SETTINGS: SAUTÉ (MEDIUM), PRESSURE COOK (HIGH)
RELEASE: NATURAL, QUICK

1 Select **Sauté (Medium),** and heat the oil, if using, in the inner pot until hot. (Otherwise, you can dry sauté in the hot pot or add a bit of water in the bottom of the pot.) Add the onion, carrots, and celery, and sauté until the onion is softened and golden, 3 to 5 minutes. Press **Cancel.**

2 Meanwhile, rinse the peas several times, picking out any debris. Add the cleaned peas, broth, salt, pepper, thyme, and bay leaves. Lock the lid and ensure the steam release valve is set to the sealing position. Select **Pressure Cook (High),** and set the cook time for **15 minutes.**

3 Once the cook time is complete, allow the pressure to release naturally for 5 minutes, then quick release any remaining pressure. Carefully remove the lid.

4 Remove the thyme stems and bay leaves. Season to taste with more salt and pepper. Serve immediately, garnished with fresh parsley.

1 tbsp extra virgin olive oil (optional)

1 yellow onion

3 carrots, peeled and diced

3 celery stalks, diced

16oz (450g) dry split peas

6 cups vegetable broth

1 tsp sea salt, plus more to taste

¼ tsp freshly ground black pepper, plus more to taste

4 sprigs fresh thyme, or ½ tsp dried thyme

2 bay leaves

½ cup chopped flat-leaf parsley, to garnish

tip *Split pea soup thickens quite a bit as it cools, but it reheats wonderfully the next day. Add a bit more broth to loosen leftovers.*

Nutrition per serving:
CALORIES: 471; **TOTAL FAT:** 5g; **SATURATED FAT:** 1g; **CHOLESTEROL:** 0mg; **SODIUM:** 1183mg; **TOTAL CARBOHYDRATE:** 81g; **FIBER:** 31g; **PROTEIN:** 29g

CLASSIC MINESTRONE SOUP
with Pesto

This minestrone recipe is quick, easy, hearty, and delicious. Serve your minestrone soup with a chunk of crusty bread for a warming Italian dinner.

 SERVES: 8

 PREP: 10 MINUTES
PRESSURE: 4 MINUTES
TOTAL: 35 MINUTES

 SETTINGS: SAUTÉ (MEDIUM),
PRESSURE COOK (HIGH)
RELEASE: QUICK

1 Select **Sauté (Medium),** and heat the oil, if using, in the inner pot until hot. (Otherwise, you can dry sauté in the hot pot or add a bit of water in the bottom of the pot.) Add the onion, garlic, carrots, celery, and butternut squash. Sauté until softened and golden, 3 to 5 minutes.

2 Add the tomatoes, broth, beans, pasta, thyme, rosemary, and oregano, and stir to combine. Lock the lid and ensure the steam release valve is set to the sealing position. Select **Pressure Cook (High),** and set the cook time for **4 minutes.**

3 Once the cook time is complete, immediately quick release the pressure. Carefully remove the lid and stir in the spinach to wilt. Season to taste with salt and pepper. Serve immediately, garnished with fresh parsley and a dollop of pesto.

1 tsp extra virgin olive oil (optional)

1 large yellow onion, diced

4 cloves garlic, minced

2 cups chopped carrots (½-in; 1.25cm pieces)

2 cups chopped celery (½-in; 1.25cm pieces)

2½ cups diced butternut squash (½-in; 1.25cm pieces)

1 (26oz; 735g) box crushed or diced tomatoes

4 cups vegetable broth

3½ cups cooked white beans, drained and rinsed

1 cup dry shell pasta (or farfalle)

1 tbsp chopped fresh thyme leaves

2 sprigs fresh rosemary, leaves chopped

1 tbsp dried oregano

5oz (140g) baby spinach (about 4 cups)

Sea salt, to taste

Freshly ground black pepper, to taste

Chopped flat-leaf parsley, for garnish

½ cup vegan pesto (store-bought or homemade), for garnish

tip *To make this dish gluten-free, simply omit the pasta. I don't recommend substituting gluten-free pasta because the cook time might be different.*

Nutrition per serving:
CALORIES: 628; **TOTAL FAT:** 14g; **SATURATED FAT:** 2g; **CHOLESTEROL:** 0mg; **SODIUM:** 1787mg; **TOTAL CARBOHYDRATE:** 105g; **FIBER:** 26g; **PROTEIN:** 30g

SERVES: 4

PREP: 5 MINUTES
PRESSURE: 2 MINUTES
TOTAL: 20 MINUTES

SETTINGS: SAUTÉ (MEDIUM),
PRESSURE COOK (HIGH)
RELEASE: QUICK

1 tbsp extra virgin olive oil
(optional)

1 yellow onion, chopped

2 celery stalks, chopped

4 cloves garlic, minced

12oz (340g) broccoli florets
(about 6 cups)

5 cups vegetable broth

1 tsp sea salt

¼ tsp freshly ground black pepper

½ cup nutritional yeast (such as
Bragg's or Trader Joe's), or to taste

⅓ cup flat-leaf parsley, plus more
for garnish

1 batch Simple Cashew Cream
(see p156)

CREAMY BROCCOLI SOUP

This creamy soup may just be the tastiest way to enjoy broccoli ever!
Nutritional yeast lends a mild cheesy note, while cashew cream makes
this simple soup rich and comforting.

1 Select **Sauté (Medium),** and heat the oil, if using, in the inner pot until
hot. (Otherwise, you can dry sauté in the hot pot or add a bit of water
in the bottom of the pot.) Add the onion and celery and sauté until
softened and golden, 3 to 5 minutes. Press **Cancel.**

2 Add the garlic, broccoli, broth, salt, and pepper. Lock the lid and
ensure the steam release valve is set to the sealing position. Select
Pressure Cook (High), and set the cook time for **2 minutes.**

3 Once the cook time is complete, immediately quick release the
pressure and carefully remove the lid. Let the soup cool slightly so it's
no longer scalding hot and carefully transfer to a blender, or use an
immersion blender. Add the nutritional yeast, parsley, and ½ cup
cashew cream. If using a stand blender, remove the center of the
lid for ventilation and cover the hole with a towel.

4 Blend until smooth. Season to taste with additional salt, pepper, and
nutritional yeast, if desired. Serve immediately, garnished with a drizzle
of additional cashew cream and fresh parsley.

Nutrition per serving:
CALORIES: 278; **TOTAL FAT:** 15g; **SATURATED FAT:** 0g; **CHOLESTEROL:** 0mg;
SODIUM: 1660mg; **TOTAL CARBOHYDRATE:** 26g; **FIBER:** 6g; **PROTEIN:** 13g

WHITE BEAN AND KALE SOUP

This hearty Italian-style soup makes a family-friendly, one-pot meal loaded with nutrition. It's full of rich flavor and umami from the broth and nutritional yeast and many textures from the variety of veggies.

 SERVES: 6

 PREP: 10 MINUTES
PRESSURE: 6 MINUTES
TOTAL: 35 MINUTES

 SETTINGS: SAUTÉ (MEDIUM), PRESSURE COOK (HIGH)
RELEASE: QUICK

1 tbsp extra virgin olive oil (optional)

1 yellow onion, diced

3 carrots, chopped

3 celery stalks, sliced

3 medium potatoes, diced

4 cloves garlic, minced

2 tbsp Italian Seasoning Blend (see p155)

1 (26oz; 735g) box crushed or diced tomatoes

3 cups cooked white beans, such as cannellini (drained if canned)

4 cups vegetable broth

2 tsp sea salt, divided

1 bunch kale, de-stemmed and chopped

½ cup nutritional yeast or vegan Parmesan cheese, plus more to serve

Freshly ground black pepper, to taste

1 Select **Sauté (Medium),** and heat the oil, if using, in the inner pot until hot. (Otherwise, you can dry sauté in the hot pot or add a bit of water in the bottom of the pot.) Add the onion and sauté until softened and golden, 3 to 5 minutes. Add the carrots, celery, potatoes, garlic, and Italian Seasoning Blend, and sauté 1 minute more. Press **Cancel.**

2 Add the tomatoes, beans, broth, and 1 teaspoon salt, and stir to combine. Lock the lid and ensure the steam release valve is set to the sealing position. Select **Pressure Cook (High),** and set the cook time for **6 minutes.**

3 Once the cook time is complete, immediately quick release the pressure and carefully remove the lid. Add the kale and stir to wilt. Stir in the nutritional yeast or Parmesan, and season to taste with pepper and the remaining 1 teaspoon salt. Serve hot with additional nutritional yeast or Parmesan.

tip *This soup is even better the next day. Take leftovers to school or work in insulated containers or jars.*

Nutrition per serving:
CALORIES: 316; **TOTAL FAT:** 3g; **SATURATED FAT:** 0g; **CHOLESTEROL:** 0mg; **SODIUM:** 817mg; **TOTAL CARBOHYDRATE:** 57g; **FIBER:** 14g; **PROTEIN:** 17g

SERVES: 4

PREP: 5 MINUTES
PRESSURE: 5 MINUTES
TOTAL: 20 MINUTES

SETTINGS: PRESSURE COOK (HIGH)
RELEASE: QUICK

1½lb (680g) carrots, peeled and cut into 1-in (2.5cm) chunks

1 tbsp freshly grated ginger

1 tsp ground turmeric

1 (13fl oz; 385ml) can light coconut milk

2–4 cups vegetable broth

¼ tsp sea salt

⅛ tsp freshly ground black pepper

1 cup microgreens (optional), to serve

6oz (170g) plain vegan yogurt (optional), to serve

CARROT GINGER SOUP

This easy soup recipe is infused with ginger and turmeric and made extra creamy with coconut milk. Flavorful carrot ginger soup is my go-to cold-busting recipe.

1 Add the carrots, ginger, turmeric, coconut milk, 2 cups vegetable broth, salt, and pepper to the inner pot. Lock the lid and ensure the steam release valve is set to the sealing position. Select **Pressure Cook (High),** and set the cook time for **5 minutes.**

2 Once the cook time is complete, immediately quick release the pressure and carefully remove the lid. Let the soup cool slightly so it's no longer scalding hot and carefully transfer to a blender, working in batches as needed, or use an immersion blender. If using a stand blender, remove the center of the lid for ventilation and cover the hole with a towel.

3 Blend on low speed until the soup is puréed. Add more broth as needed to thin. Add more salt, pepper, and grated ginger to taste.

4 Pour directly from the blender into bowls, or place back into the pot on **Warm** mode. Garnish with microgreens and more coconut milk or plain yogurt, if desired.

Nutrition per serving:
CALORIES: 169; **TOTAL FAT:** 7g; **SATURATED FAT:** 5g; **CHOLESTEROL:** 0mg; **SODIUM:** 474mg; **TOTAL CARBOHYDRATE:** 24g; **FIBER:** 5g; **PROTEIN:** 3g

SALADS & SIDES

BEET SALAD
with Orange Vinaigrette

Steamed beets, perfect for prepping on the weekend and enjoying all week, are one of my favorites to make in the Instant Pot—they're done so much faster than roasting in the oven. Use them to make this elegant beet and citrus salad.

1 Fill the inner pot with the trivet, steam rack, or a steamer basket, and add 1 cup water. Place the beets on the trivet. Lock the lid and ensure the steam release valve is set to the sealing position. Select **Pressure Cook (High),** and set the cook time for **15 to 20 minutes,** depending on the size of the beets.

2 Once the cook time is complete, immediately quick release the pressure. Carefully remove the lid and make sure the beets are fork-tender. If not, lock the lid and pressure cook for 3 to 5 minutes more.

3 Allow the beets to cool enough to handle. Slip the skins off under cool running water and discard. Cut the beets into rounds or wedges.

4 Meanwhile, make the dressing. Place all ingredients except the olive oil in a blender. Blend until the shallot is very finely chopped. Slowly blend in the olive oil.

5 In a large salad bowl, toss the arugula with the desired amount of dressing. Arrange orange segments and beet pieces on top. Sprinkle with walnuts and cheese. (Don't toss this all together because the beets will turn the whole salad pink.) Serve immediately.

 SERVES: 6

 PREP: 10 MINUTES
PRESSURE: 20 MINUTES
TOTAL: 45 MINUTES

 SETTINGS: PRESSURE COOK (HIGH)
RELEASE: QUICK

1 cup water

4 medium beets

5oz (140g) arugula (about 4 cups)

2 navel oranges, peeled and sliced

½ cup raw walnuts

¼ cup crumbled vegan goat-style cheese (such as Treeline, Miyoko's, or Kite Hill)

FOR THE DRESSING:

1 small shallot, cut into large chunks

1 clove garlic, minced

⅓ cup freshly squeezed orange juice

Zest of 1 orange

2 tbsp balsamic vinegar or red wine vinegar

¼ tsp sea salt

¼ tsp freshly ground black pepper

½ tsp Dijon mustard

Squeeze of fresh lemon

1 tbsp agave syrup

¼ cup extra virgin olive oil

tip *You can use your favorite store-bought or homemade vinaigrette with this recipe. Balsamic or champagne vinaigrette would both work.*

You can cut up the cooked beets and drizzle with a little balsamic for a warm side dish.

Nutrition per serving:
CALORIES: 208; **TOTAL FAT:** 14g; **SATURATED FAT:** 3g; **CHOLESTEROL:** 0mg; **SODIUM:** 138mg; **TOTAL CARBOHYDRATE:** 19g; **FIBER:** 3g; **PROTEIN:** 3g

TABBOULEH

SERVES: 6

PREP: 15 MINUTES
PRESSURE: 12 MINUTES
TOTAL: 45 MINUTES

SETTINGS: RICE (LOW)
RELEASE: QUICK

1 cup uncooked coarse bulgur wheat (such as Bob's Red Mill Red Bulgur)

2 cups water

2 tbsp extra virgin olive oil

3 cups finely chopped flat-leaf parsley (3 bunches)

½ cup finely chopped fresh mint

2 Persian cucumbers, chopped into ½-in (1.25cm) pieces

1pt (551ml) rainbow cherry tomatoes, halved

¼ cup fresh lemon juice

½ tsp sea salt

¼ tsp ground cumin

Freshly ground black pepper, to taste

Loaded with fresh herbs, crunchy cucumber, and juicy tomatoes, classic tabbouleh is delicious as a side salad, stuffed in pita pockets with hummus, or as part of a mezze platter. For a gluten-free option, swap the bulgur for Perfect Quinoa (see p117).

1 Add the bulgur wheat and 2 cups water to the inner pot. Lock the lid and ensure the steam release valve is set to the sealing position. Select **Rice (Low),** and set the cook time for **12 minutes.**

2 Once the cook time is complete, immediately quick release the pressure. Carefully remove the lid and stir the bulgur. Transfer to a large salad bowl and dress with the olive oil to help separate the grains. Allow the bulgur to cool completely. You can place the bowl in the freezer for a few minutes to speed up cooling.

3 Add all remaining ingredients to the bulgur, and toss gently to combine. Season to taste with any additional salt, pepper, and lemon juice.

4 Refrigerate until ready to serve. This salad tastes best after it's chilled for a few hours.

tip *You can switch up this recipe by adding 1½ cups cooked chickpeas for a protein boost or swapping the tomatoes for pomegranate arils in the winter.*

Nutrition per serving:
CALORIES: 158; **TOTAL FAT:** 6g; **SATURATED FAT:** 0g; **CHOLESTEROL:** 0mg; **SODIUM:** 340mg; **TOTAL CARBOHYDRATE:** 26g; **FIBER:** 7g; **PROTEIN:** 5g

ITALIAN FARRO SALAD

Farro has been an Italian staple since ancient Roman times. It's a hearty, chewy, nutty grain that is great for soups and salads. This simple tomato and farro salad is commonly found in cafés throughout Tuscany.

SERVES: 6

PREP: 15 MINUTES
PRESSURE: 17 MINUTES
TOTAL: 40 MINUTES

SETTINGS: PRESSURE COOK (HIGH)
RELEASE: NATURAL, QUICK

1 Add the farro and 3 cups water to the inner pot. Lock the lid and ensure the steam release valve is set to the sealing position. Select **Pressure Cook (High),** and set the cook time for **17 minutes.**

2 Once the cook time is complete, allow the pressure to release naturally for 10 minutes, then quick release any remaining pressure. Carefully remove the lid and transfer the cooked farro to a sieve and rinse with cold water to stop the cooking.

3 To prepare the salad, add the diced tomatoes, onion, bell pepper, and basil to a salad bowl. Add the cooked and cooled farro, and toss to combine.

4 In a small bowl, whisk together the olive oil, balsamic vinegar, and garlic. Dress the farro salad with the vinaigrette and season to taste with salt and pepper. Serve the farro salad immediately on plates or in bowls over a bed of lettuce, drizzled with a bit more oil and vinegar.

1 cup farro, rinsed and drained (see tip)

3 cups water

4 Roma tomatoes, deseeded and diced

½ yellow onion, diced

1 yellow bell pepper, deseeded and diced

1 medium bunch fresh basil, leaves thinly sliced

¼ cup extra virgin olive oil, plus more for serving

¼ cup balsamic vinegar, plus more for serving

1 clove garlic, minced

Sea salt, to taste

Freshly ground black pepper, to taste

5oz (140g) baby lettuce mix (about 4 cups), for serving

tip *There are several varieties of farro on the market, from traditional whole farro to quick-cooking or semi-perlato. I recommend Bob's Red Mill Organic Farro. If using semi-perlato, cook on high pressure for 6 minutes with 2 cups water.*

Nutrition per serving:
CALORIES: 206; **TOTAL FAT:** 10g; **SATURATED FAT:** 1g; **CHOLESTEROL:** 0mg;
SODIUM: 70mg; **TOTAL CARBOHYDRATE:** 27g; **FIBER:** 3g; **PROTEIN:** 4g

SERVES: 6

 PREP: 10 MINUTES, PLUS OVERNIGHT FOR SOAKING
PRESSURE: 12 MINUTES
TOTAL: 40 MINUTES

 SETTINGS: PRESSURE COOK (HIGH)
RELEASE: NATURAL

---

1 cup dried chickpeas, soaked overnight

4 cups water

1 tbsp extra virgin olive oil

3 tbsp red wine vinegar

2 tbsp freshly squeezed lemon juice

1 clove garlic, minced

1pt (551ml) cherry tomatoes, quartered

½ small red onion, diced

½ cup pitted Kalamata olive halves

½ cup chopped flat-leaf parsley

Sea salt, to taste

Freshly ground black pepper, to taste

BALELA

This flavorful Middle Eastern salad with tomatoes, onions, and olives is tastier than ever made with freshly cooked chickpeas. It's perfect for meal prep because it stays fresh for several days.

1 Drain and rinse the chickpeas, and add them to the inner pot. Add 4 cups water. There should be an inch or two of water covering the beans; if not, add more.

2 Lock the lid and ensure the steam release valve is set to the sealing position. Select **Pressure Cook (High),** and set the cook time for **12 minutes.**

3 Once the cook time is complete, allow the pressure to release naturally. Carefully remove the lid and make sure the beans are tender. If not, lock the lid and pressure cook for 3 minutes more.

4 Drain the beans and transfer to a medium bowl. Immediately toss with the olive oil, vinegar, lemon juice, and garlic so they don't dry out. Let cool to room temperature.

5 Add the tomatoes, onion, olives, and parsley. Toss to combine. Season to taste with salt and pepper. Enjoy immediately, or store covered in the refrigerator for up to 4 days.

tip *Skip the olive oil to make this dish oil-free.*

For a beautiful presentation, serve the salad in romaine leaves.
It could be eaten as a lettuce wrap or with a fork and knife.

Nutrition per serving:
CALORIES: 170; **TOTAL FAT:** 6g; **SATURATED FAT:** 1g; **CHOLESTEROL:** 0mg; **SODIUM:** 159mg; **TOTAL CARBOHYDRATE:** 24g; **FIBER:** 7g; **PROTEIN:** 7g

SERVES: 6

 PREP: 10 MINUTES
PRESSURE: 33 MINUTES, PLUS
1 MINUTE
TOTAL: 1 HOUR 20 MINUTES

 SETTINGS: PRESSURE COOK (HIGH)
RELEASE: NATURAL, QUICK

1 cup dried chickpeas, rinsed

5 cups water, divided

1 cup quinoa, rinsed

¼ tsp sea salt

½ small red onion, halved
and thinly sliced

5 strawberries, sliced

2 Persian cucumbers, diced

1 small bunch flat-leaf parsley,
chopped

3 cups chopped baby spinach
or arugula

1 avocado

FOR THE VINAIGRETTE:

3 tbsp extra virgin olive oil

¼ cup apple cider vinegar

1 clove garlic, minced

1 tbsp pure maple syrup

1 tbsp Dijon mustard

½ tsp sea salt

STRAWBERRY CHICKPEA QUINOA SALAD

This hearty, sweet, and savory salad features vibrant colors, a variety of textures, and plenty of satiating protein from the quinoa and fat from the avocado. It makes a great lunch or light dinner.

1   Add the chickpeas and 4 cups water to the inner pot. Lock the lid and ensure the steam release valve is set to the sealing position. Select **Pressure Cook (High),** and set the cook time for **33 minutes.**

2   Once the cook time is complete, allow the pressure to release naturally for 10 minutes, then quick release any remaining pressure. Carefully remove the lid.

3   Place the trivet or steam rack in the pot on top of the chickpeas. In an oven-safe dish, add the quinoa, salt, and remaining 1 cup water. Place the dish on the trivet. Lock the lid and ensure the steam release valve is set to the sealing position. Select **Pressure Cook (High),** and set the cook time for **1 minute.**

4   Once the cook time is complete, allow the pressure to release naturally.

5   Carefully remove the lid, dish, and trivet. Transfer the quinoa to a salad bowl. Drain the chickpeas and rinse with cold water to speed up cooling. Add the drained chickpeas to the bowl of quinoa, and let cool.

6   Add the onion, strawberries, cucumbers, parsley, and spinach, and toss gently to combine.

7   To make the vinaigrette, in a small bowl, whisk together all ingredients. Toss the salad in the desired amount of dressing. Just before serving, pit and slice the avocado and place on top. Eat immediately, or cover and refrigerate for up to 1 day.

tip *While strawberries are wonderful for warmer months, the arils from one pomegranate, or one diced apple, are great swaps for colder months.*

Nutrition per serving:
CALORIES: 326; **TOTAL FAT:** 14g; **SATURATED FAT:** 2g; **CHOLESTEROL:** 0mg;
SODIUM: 169mg; **TOTAL CARBOHYDRATE:** 44g; **FIBER:** 10g; **PROTEIN:** 11g

MEDITERRANEAN LENTIL SALAD

This is a hearty Mediterranean lentil salad loaded with flavor, color, and texture from the briny olives, crunchy veggies, and creamy, dairy-free cheese. The cold salad is perfect as a light dinner or packed lunch.

SERVES: 6

PREP: 10 MINUTES
PRESSURE: 8 MINUTES
TOTAL: 30 MINUTES

SETTINGS: PRESSURE COOK (HIGH)
RELEASE: NATURAL, QUICK

1. Pick through the lentils and discard any debris or little stones. Rinse with cold water and drain. Add the lentils and 1½ cups water to the inner pot. Lock the lid and ensure the steam release valve is set to the sealing position. Select **Pressure Cook (High),** and set the cook time for **8 minutes.**

2. Once the cook time is complete, allow the pressure to release naturally for 5 minutes, then quick release any remaining pressure. Carefully remove the lid. Drain the lentils and let cool to room temperature.

3. To make the dressing, in a small bowl or jar, whisk together all ingredients. The dressing will probably separate and need whisking again before dressing the salad.

4. In a large salad bowl, arrange the lentils, tomatoes, cucumber, bell pepper, olives, onion, cheese, and parsley. Dress with the desired amount of vinaigrette. Cover and refrigerate to chill, or enjoy immediately.

¾ cup dried green lentils

1½ cups water

1 cup cherry tomatoes, halved

1 cup sliced Persian cucumbers

1 cup diced red or yellow bell peppers

½ cup halved Kalamata olives

1 small red onion, thinly sliced

½ cup crumbled dairy-free soft cheese (such as Treeline, Kite Hill, Heidi Ho, or Miyoko's) (optional)

¼ cup chopped flat leaf parsley

FOR THE DRESSING:

¼ cup extra virgin olive oil

3 tbsp red wine vinegar

Juice of ½ lemon

1 tsp Dijon mustard

1 tsp dried oregano

½ tsp sea salt

tip *Lentils don't need to be soaked, and they cook much more quickly than beans. Cook time may vary, however, depending on the size and age of the lentils. Shoot for the minimum cook time to avoid mushy lentils.*

Nutrition per serving:
CALORIES: 244; **TOTAL FAT:** 15g; **SATURATED FAT:** 4g; **CHOLESTEROL:** 0mg;
SODIUM: 117mg; **TOTAL CARBOHYDRATE:** 20g; **FIBER:** 9g; **PROTEIN:** 8g

SOUTHWESTERN BLACK BEAN AND RICE SALAD

A fiesta of colors, textures, and flavors, this hearty Southwest-inspired bean and rice salad is perfect for meal prep or potlucks.

 SERVES: 6

 PREP: 5 MINUTES
PRESSURE: 25 MINUTES
TOTAL: 1 HOUR

 SETTINGS: PRESSURE COOK (HIGH)
RELEASE: NATURAL, QUICK

1 Add the beans and 2½ cups water to the inner pot. Place the trivet over the beans.

2 In an oven-safe bowl or baking dish, such as Pyrex, add the rice, the remaining ½ cup water, and a pinch of salt. Place the dish on the trivet.

3 Lock the lid and ensure the steam release valve is set to the sealing position. Select **Pressure Cook (High),** and set the cook time for **25 minutes.**

4 Once the cook time is complete, allow the pressure to release naturally for 15 minutes, then quick release any remaining pressure. Carefully remove the lid and take the dish of rice off the trivet. Remove the trivet.

5 Transfer the rice to a large salad bowl and fluff with a fork. Drain the beans in a colander and rinse with cold water. Transfer the beans to the salad bowl.

6 Add the corn kernels, bell peppers, tomatoes, onion, lime juice, vinegar, garlic, cumin, and cilantro. Toss to combine. Season to taste with salt. Top with avocado just before eating. Enjoy warm or refrigerate until ready to eat.

1 cup dry black beans, picked over and rinsed

3 cups water, divided

½ cup long-grain brown rice, rinsed

1 ear corn, kernels cut off

1 green bell pepper, deseeded and diced

1pt (551ml) cherry tomatoes, halved

½ cup diced red onion

Juice of 1 lime

1 tbsp red wine vinegar

1 clove garlic, minced

1 tsp ground cumin

1 cup chopped fresh cilantro

½ tsp sea salt

1 avocado, diced

tip *This recipe is delicious as a side salad or stuffed inside lettuce wraps with avocado. It's also terrific with diced nectarines in the summer.*

Nutrition per serving:
CALORIES: 285; **TOTAL FAT:** 8g; **SATURATED FAT:** 1.5g; **CHOLESTEROL:** 0mg; **SODIUM:** 208mg; **TOTAL CARBOHYDRATE:** 46g; **FIBER:** 10g; **PROTEIN:** 11g

SERVES: 4

 PREP: 5 MINUTES
PRESSURE: 3 MINUTES
TOTAL: 20 MINUTES

 SETTINGS: SAUTÉ (LOW), PRESSURE COOK (LOW)
RELEASE: QUICK

1 large bunch kale
(about 10oz; 285g)

2 tbsp extra virgin olive oil

6 cloves garlic, thinly sliced crosswise

½ cup vegetable broth

¼ tsp sea salt

Freshly ground black pepper, to taste

GARLICKY BRAISED KALE

This easy and flavorful leafy green side dish goes wonderfully with almost any main dish. I love it with Creamy Polenta (see p112) and Ratatouille (see p104), or with pasta and Tempeh Bolognese (see p60).

1 Remove and discard the middle stems from the kale, and roughly chop the leafy parts. Rinse and drain the kale.

2 Select **Sauté (Low),** and heat the oil in the inner pot. Add the garlic and sauté for about 2 minutes until tender and golden, taking care not to burn it. Press **Cancel.** Transfer the garlic and oil to a small bowl and set aside.

3 Add the broth to the inner pot. Place the kale on top and sprinkle with salt and pepper. Lock the lid and ensure the steam release valve is set to the sealing position. Select **Pressure Cook (Low),** and set the cook time for **3 minutes.**

4 Once the cook time is complete, immediately quick release the pressure. Carefully remove the lid. Return the garlic and oil to the inner pot, and toss to combine. Serve immediately.

tip *Liquid is needed to bring the pot to pressure. You can reduce the liquid left over after cooking by simmering on Sauté mode for a couple of minutes or simply serving the garlic kale with a slotted spoon.*

Nutrition per serving:
CALORIES: 104; **TOTAL FAT:** 7g; **SATURATED FAT:** 1g; **CHOLESTEROL:** 0mg;
SODIUM: 286mg; **TOTAL CARBOHYDRATE:** 9g; **FIBER:** 1.5g; **PROTEIN:** 2g

BRUSSELS SPROUTS
with Balsamic Glaze

These Brussels sprouts are steamed and then seared, so they're perfectly tender on the inside without getting mushy. Tangy sweet balsamic glaze adds another layer of flavor.

 SERVES: 4

 PREP: 5 MINUTES
PRESSURE: 1 MINUTE
TOTAL: 15 MINUTES

 SETTINGS: PRESSURE COOK (HIGH), SAUTÉ (HIGH)
RELEASE: QUICK

1 Trim a thin slice off the bottom of the Brussels sprouts and remove a few outer leaves from each. Fit the inner pot with a steamer basket, and add 1 cup water. Add the Brussels sprouts to the steamer basket.

2 Lock the lid and ensure the steam release valve is set to the sealing position. Select **Pressure Cook (High),** and set the cook time for **1 minute.**

3 Once the cook time is complete, immediately quick release the pressure. Carefully remove the lid and the steamer basket. Discard the water in the inner pot and place the inner pot back in the Instant Pot.

4 Select **Sauté (High).** When the pot is hot, add the oil. Once sizzling, add the steamed Brussels sprouts and season with salt and pepper. Turn occasionally with tongs or a spatula, until seared, about 3 minutes.

5 Meanwhile, make the balsamic glaze. Pour the balsamic vinegar into a small saucepan over medium-low heat. Simmer until the vinegar is reduced and syrupy and coats the back of a spoon, 5 to 10 minutes.

6 Serve the Brussels sprouts hot with a small bowl of the balsamic glaze on the side for drizzling.

14oz (400g) whole medium-sized Brussels sprouts

1 cup water

1 tbsp extra virgin olive oil

Sea salt, to taste

Freshly ground black pepper, to taste

½ cup balsamic vinegar

tip *I like to serve the balsamic glaze on the side for anyone (especially young children) who may prefer their Brussels sprouts simply seasoned with salt and pepper.*

Nutrition per serving:
CALORIES: 79; **TOTAL FAT:** 4g; **SATURATED FAT:** 0.5g; **CHOLESTEROL:** 0mg; SODIUM: 143mg; **TOTAL CARBOHYDRATE:** 9g; **FIBER:** 4g; **PROTEIN:** 3g

SERVES: 4

PREP: 15 MINUTES
PRESSURE: 25 MINUTES
TOTAL: 55 MINUTES

SETTINGS: SAUTÉ (MEDIUM), PRESSURE COOK (HIGH)
RELEASE: QUICK

1 cup water

1 zucchini, thinly sliced crosswise

1 yellow summer squash, thinly sliced crosswise

1 Japanese eggplant, thinly sliced crosswise

2 Roma tomatoes, thinly sliced crosswise

Pinch of sea salt

Pinch of freshly ground black pepper

Fresh thyme leaves, for garnish

½ cup chopped fresh basil leaves, for garnish

FOR THE SAUCE:

1 tbsp extra virgin olive oil (optional)

1 small shallot, chopped

1 clove garlic, minced

1 tsp fresh thyme leaves

1 (15oz; 420g) can crushed tomatoes

¼ tsp sea salt

FOR THE VINAIGRETTE:

1 tbsp extra virgin olive oil

1 tbsp balsamic vinegar

1 clove garlic, minced

RATATOUILLE

This swirled Ratatouille is as delicious as it is beautiful. Delicate tomato sauce, fresh herbs, and a simple vinaigrette infuse tender summer vegetables with flavor in this French-inspired recipe.

1 To make the sauce, select **Sauté (Medium),** and heat the oil, if using, in the inner pot until hot. (Otherwise, you can dry sauté in the hot pot, or add a bit of water in the bottom of the pot.) Add the shallot and sauté until softened, about 2 minutes. Add the garlic and thyme, and sauté 1 minute more, taking care not to burn the garlic or shallot. Add the tomatoes and salt. Simmer for 5 minutes, stirring occasionally, until the sauce has thickened slightly. Press **Cancel.**

2 Spread ¾ cup sauce in the bottom of a 7-inch (17.5cm) oven-safe baking dish. Save the remaining sauce for serving. Rinse the inner pot and place it back in the Instant Pot. Fit the inner pot with the trivet, and add 1 cup water.

3 Arrange the zucchini, yellow squash, eggplant, and tomato slices vertically in the sauce, alternating colors, around the perimeter of the dish. Continue until you've reached the center.

4 Season the vegetables with a pinch of salt and pepper. Cover the dish with foil, and place on the trivet. Lock the lid and ensure the steam release valve is set to the sealing position. Select **Pressure Cook (High),** and set the cook time for **25 minutes.**

5 Once the cook time is complete, immediately quick release the pressure. Carefully remove the lid and dish. Remove the foil. Garnish with fresh thyme and basil leaves.

6 Meanwhile, make the vinaigrette. Whisk all ingredients until combined. Enjoy the vegetables immediately with the vinaigrette drizzled over and more sauce, if desired.

 Ratatouille is lovely served with creamy polenta, rice, or pasta.

Nutrition per serving:
CALORIES: 116; **TOTAL FAT:** 4g; **SATURATED FAT:** 0.5g; **CHOLESTEROL:** 0mg; **SODIUM:** 255mg; **TOTAL CARBOHYDRATE:** 19g; **FIBER:** 9g; **PROTEIN:** 5g

MAKES: ABOUT 4 CUPS

PREP: 10 MINUTES
PRESSURE: 6 MINUTES
TOTAL: 40 MINUTES

SETTINGS: PRESSURE COOK (HIGH)
RELEASE: NATURAL, QUICK

3lb (1.5kg) apples, peeled and quartered

1 tbsp fresh lemon juice

½ cup water

OPTIONAL ADDITIONS:

Winter: 1½ cups fresh or frozen cranberries

Spring: 1½ cups fresh or frozen blackberries

Summer: 1½ cups fresh or frozen peach slices

Autumn: 2 cinnamon sticks

APPLESAUCE FOR EVERY SEASON

Homemade applesauce is so much tastier than store-bought and takes just a few minutes to prepare. From classic to flavored, here are applesauce varieties for all four seasons.

1 Add the apples, lemon juice, and ½ cup water to the inner pot. Add any of the optional additions, if desired. Lock the lid and ensure the steam release valve is set to the sealing position. Select **Pressure Cook (High),** and set the cook time for **6 minutes.**

2 Once the cook time is complete, allow the pressure to release naturally for 10 minutes, then quick release any remaining pressure. Carefully remove the lid. Use a potato masher to mash the apples to your desired consistency.

3 Transfer to a lidded glass storage container. Enjoy warm or cold. Store in the refrigerator for up to 10 days.

tip *You can make this as a half batch if preferred. Quick release immediately when the cook time is complete—there is less applesauce, so it won't sputter out of the valve the way it does with a full batch.*

Nutrition per ½ cup (excluding optional additions):
CALORIES: 54; **TOTAL FAT:** 0g; **SATURATED FAT:** 0g; **CHOLESTEROL:** 0mg; **SODIUM:** 0mg; **TOTAL CARBOHYDRATE:** 14g; **FIBER:** 2g; **PROTEIN:** 0g

ROSEMARY ROASTED BABY POTATOES

Roasting potatoes has never been quicker or easier! These delicious little potatoes are soft on the inside and crisp on the outside, and coated with earthy rosemary, garlic, and olive oil.

 SERVES: 4

 PREP: 2 MINUTES
PRESSURE: 3 MINUTES
TOTAL: 15 MINUTES

 SETTINGS: PRESSURE COOK (HIGH), SAUTÉ (HIGH)
RELEASE: QUICK

1 Fit the inner pot with a steamer basket. Rinse the potatoes and add them to the basket. Add 1 cup water.

2 Lock the lid and ensure the steam release valve is set to the sealing position. Select **Pressure Cook (High)**, and set the cook time for **3 minutes.**

3 Once the cook time is complete, immediately quick release the pressure and carefully remove the lid. If the potatoes are not completely tender, cook for 2 minutes more, or until tender. Remove the steamer basket. Using potholders, discard the cooking water from the inner pot. Place the inner pot back into the Instant Pot.

4 Select **Sauté (High),** and heat the oil until very hot and sizzling. Add the potatoes and sauté for 3 to 5 minutes to crisp up the skin. Press **Cancel.** Add the rosemary and garlic, and sauté 1 minute more.

5 Season the potatoes to taste with salt and pepper. Transfer to a serving bowl and enjoy warm.

1lb (450g) 1-in (2.5cm) baby potatoes

1 cup water

1 tbsp extra virgin olive oil

1 tbsp chopped fresh rosemary leaves

1 clove garlic, minced

Sea salt, to taste

Freshly ground black pepper, to taste

tip *Cook time may vary depending on the size of your potatoes. If yours are larger than 1 inch (2.5cm), you may want to add another minute or two.*

Nutrition per serving:
CALORIES: 119; **TOTAL FAT:** 4g; **SATURATED FAT:** 1g; **CHOLESTEROL:** 0mg; **SODIUM:** 77mg; **TOTAL CARBOHYDRATE:** 20g; **FIBER:** 3g; **PROTEIN:** 2g

SERVES: 4

 PREP: 5 MINUTES
PRESSURE: 3 MINUTES
TOTAL: 15 MINUTES

 SETTINGS: PRESSURE COOK (HIGH),
SAUTÉ (MEDIUM)
RELEASE: QUICK

1 cup water

4 cups peeled sweet potato chunks
(2-in; 5-cm pieces; about 2lb)

3 tbsp vegan butter (such as
Miyoko's or Earth Balance)

4 sage leaves, thinly sliced

Sea salt, to taste

Freshly ground black pepper,
to taste

SAGE SWEET POTATO MASH

Fresh sage leaves add beautiful earthiness and contrast to mashed sweet potatoes. This recipe makes a quick and easy weeknight side dish but is just as at home on your holiday dinner table.

1   Fit the inner pot with a steamer basket, and add 1 cup water. Place the sweet potato chunks into the basket. Lock the lid and ensure the steam release valve is set to the sealing position. Select **Pressure Cook (High),** and set the cook time for **3 minutes.**

2   Once the cook time is complete, immediately quick release the pressure. Carefully remove the lid and ensure sweet potatoes are very tender. If not, lock the lid and pressure cook for 1 minute more, or until tender. Use tongs to carefully remove the steamer basket and potatoes. Discard the water and return the inner pot to the Instant Pot.

3   Select **Sauté (Medium),** and melt the butter. Sauté the sage leaves until fragrant, about 2 minutes. Add the sweet potatoes to the pot and mash with a potato masher to the desired consistency. Season to taste with salt and pepper. Serve immediately.

tip   *This easy recipe makes a wonderful holiday side dish or topping for Shepherd-Less Pie (see p49).*

Nutrition per serving:
CALORIES: 151; **TOTAL FAT:** 4g; **SATURATED FAT:** 1g; **CHOLESTEROL:** 0mg;
SODIUM: 204mg; **TOTAL CARBOHYDRATE:** 27g; **FIBER:** 4g; **PROTEIN:** 2g

TRUFFLED OLIVE OIL MASHED POTATOES

These mashed potatoes are decadently flavored with garlic, olive oil, and truffles, so you won't miss the dairy.

 SERVES: 6

 PREP: 10 MINUTES
PRESSURE: 8 MINUTES
TOTAL: 30 MINUTES

 SETTINGS: PRESSURE COOK (HIGH)
RELEASE: QUICK

1 Add the potatoes, garlic, and 1 cup plus 2 tablespoons water to the inner pot. Lock the lid and ensure the steam release valve is set to the sealing position. Select **Pressure Cook (High),** and set the cook time for **8 minutes.**

2 Once the cook time is complete, immediately quick release the pressure and carefully remove the lid. The potatoes should be tender with just a little water remaining in the pot. If potatoes are not yet tender, put the lid back on and pressure cook for 2 minutes more.

3 Use a potato masher to mash the potatoes and garlic. Whisk or stir in the olive oil and truffle salt.

2lb (1kg) peeled Yukon Gold potatoes (about 5 medium), cut into 2-in (5cm) pieces

8 cloves garlic, peeled

1 cup, plus 2 tbsp water

¼ cup extra virgin olive oil

1 tsp truffle salt

tip *For even richer flavor, mash in a few cloves of roasted garlic (see p123) instead of cooking with the raw garlic.*

You can find truffle salt in Italian grocery stores and gourmet shops, but it's even more affordably priced online.

Nutrition per serving:
CALORIES: 190; **TOTAL FAT:** 9g; **SATURATED FAT:** 1g; **CHOLESTEROL:** 0mg; **SODIUM:** 212mg; **TOTAL CARBOHYDRATE:** 25g; **FIBER:** 4g; **PROTEIN:** 3g

SALADS & SIDES   109

WHOLE ROASTED CAULIFLOWER
with Garlic and Herb Crust

Roasting a whole cauliflower traditionally takes about an hour. With this simple Instant Pot method, it takes just minutes! Packed with flavor and crunch, this dish is like the vegetable version of garlic bread. Serve as a side dish, or as a main on a bed of sweet potato mash.

 SERVES: 4 AS A SIDE DISH

 PREP: 5 MINUTES
PRESSURE: 0 MINUTES
TOTAL: 25 MINUTES

 SETTINGS: PRESSURE COOK (HIGH)
RELEASE: QUICK

1   Rinse and pat the cauliflower dry. Cut off the leaves, but do not remove much of the stem, or the florets may fall off. Preheat the oven to 450°F (230°C).

2   Add 1 cup water and the salt to the inner pot. Fit the inner pot with a steamer basket, and place the whole cauliflower, stem-side down, into the basket. Lock the lid and ensure the steam release valve is set to the sealing position. Select **Pressure Cook (High),** and set the cook time for **0 minutes.** (Even though the pressure cooking time is 0 minutes, the cauliflower cooks perfectly during the time it takes the pot to come to pressure.)

3   Immediately quick release the pressure. Carefully remove the lid and set the cauliflower in a casserole dish.

4   In a small bowl, stir together the melted butter and garlic. Turn the cauliflower upside down and brush with garlic butter (about ½ tablespoon). Turn the cauliflower right side up and brush with the remaining garlic butter. Press the bread crumbs and parsley firmly onto the cauliflower, creating a crust and ensuring the bread crumbs are moistened with butter. (Some bread crumbs will fall to the bottom, which will be used later for serving.)

5   Transfer to the oven and roast for 5 to 10 minutes until the bread crumbs are golden brown, checking often for burning. If the top of the cauliflower gets too brown, cover with a small piece of foil to allow the rest of the cauliflower and the crumbs at the bottom of the dish to brown.

6   Season with a pinch of salt and pepper. Cut into slices. Serve the slices immediately, topped with additional toasted garlic bread crumbs from the bottom of the dish.

1 medium whole cauliflower

1 cup water

3 tbsp sea salt

4½ tbsp melted, salted vegan butter (such as Miyoko's)

3 cloves garlic, minced

¾ cup plain panko bread crumbs (gluten-free bread crumbs, if needed)

¼ cup chopped flat-leaf parsley

Sea salt, to taste

Freshly ground black pepper, to taste

tip *Be sure to choose a cauliflower that will fit in your Instant Pot steamer basket. Seven inches (17½cm) across is perfect for a 6-quart (5.5l) Instant Pot.*

Nutrition per serving:
CALORIES: 229; **TOTAL FAT:** 12g; **SATURATED FAT:** 3g; **CHOLESTEROL:** 0mg; **SODIUM:** 415mg; **TOTAL CARBOHYDRATE:** 26g; **PROTEIN:** 7g; **FIBER:** 5g

CREAMY POLENTA

SERVES: 6

PREP: 1 MINUTE
PRESSURE: 7 MINUTES
TOTAL: 30 MINUTES

SETTINGS: PRESSURE COOK (HIGH)
RELEASE: NATURAL, QUICK

4 cups water

1 cup uncooked polenta

½ tsp sea salt

Freshly ground black pepper, to taste

½ cup shredded vegan Parmesan cheese (such as Follow Your Heart)

This comforting Italian side dish traditionally requires constant attention and stirring but takes just a minute of prep in the Instant Pot. It's lovely as a side to accompany ratatouille or as a base for sautéed mushrooms or greens.

1 Add 4 cups water to the inner pot. Gently sprinkle the polenta, salt, and a pinch of pepper over the water, without stirring. If stirred, the polenta will often trigger the burn warning on the Instant Pot.

2 Lock the lid and ensure the steam release valve is set to the sealing position. Select **Pressure Cook (High),** and set the cook time for **7 minutes.**

3 Once the cook time is complete, allow the pressure to release naturally for 10 minutes, then quick release any remaining pressure. Whisk until smooth and stir in the Parmesan. Season to taste with additional salt and pepper. The polenta will firm up as it cools, but if it doesn't seem cooked enough, put the lid back on and let it sit for 10 minutes more.

4 Serve warm right away because polenta will solidify if left at room temperature too long.

tip *It's important to use traditional coarse (rather than instant) polenta for this recipe. I recommend Bob's Red Mill Organic Polenta Corn Grits.*

Nutrition per serving:
CALORIES: 113; **TOTAL FAT:** 3.5g; **SATURATED FAT:** 2g; **CHOLESTEROL:** 0mg; **SODIUM:** 181mg; **TOTAL CARBOHYDRATE:** 18g; **FIBER:** 1.5g; **PROTEIN:** 2g

BAKED BEANS

Savory, sweet baked beans are a classic BBQ side dish. Serve warm from the Instant Pot with veggie burgers, coleslaw, and corn on the cob for the ultimate American summer meal.

 SERVES: 4

 PREP: 5 MINUTES
PRESSURE: 25 MINUTES, PLUS 5 MINUTES
TOTAL: 1 HOUR 10 MINUTES

 SETTINGS: PRESSURE COOK (HIGH), SAUTÉ (MEDIUM)
RELEASE: NATURAL, QUICK

1 cup dried pinto beans, rinsed

4⅔ cups water, divided

1 tbsp extra virgin olive oil (optional)

1 yellow onion, diced

¼ cup ketchup

1 tbsp vegan Worcestershire sauce (gluten-free, if needed) (see tip)

1 tbsp Dijon mustard

1 tbsp pure maple syrup

1 tbsp molasses

½ tsp sea salt

¼ tsp freshly ground black pepper

1 Add the beans and 4 cups water to the inner pot. Lock the lid and ensure the steam release valve is set to the sealing position. Select **Pressure Cook (High),** and set the cook time for **25 minutes.**

2 Once the cook time is complete, allow the pressure to release naturally for 15 minutes, then quick release any remaining pressure. Press **Cancel**. Carefully remove the lid and drain the beans in a colander. Rinse the beans with cold water.

3 Place the inner pot back into the Instant Pot. Select **Sauté (Medium),** and heat the oil, if using, in the inner pot until hot. (Otherwise, you can dry sauté in the hot pot or add a bit of water in the bottom of the pot.) Add the onion and sauté until softened and golden, 3 to 5 minutes. Press **Cancel.** Add the remaining ⅔ cup water to deglaze the pan, using a wooden spoon to scrape up any bits stuck to the bottom.

4 Add the beans back to the inner pot, along with the ketchup, Worcestershire sauce, mustard, syrup, molasses, salt, and pepper. Stir to combine.

5 Lock the lid and ensure the steam release valve is set to the sealing position. Select **Pressure Cook (High),** and set the cook time for **5 minutes.**

6 Once the cook time is complete, allow the pressure to release naturally for 5 minutes, then quick release any remaining pressure. Carefully remove the lid and select **Warm** until ready to eat. Ladle the beans into bowls and serve.

tip *Traditional Worcestershire sauce is neither gluten-free nor vegan. Most natural foods stores now carry brands like Annie's (vegan) and Robbie's (gluten-free and vegan).*

Nutrition per serving:
CALORIES: 243; **TOTAL FAT:** 3g; **SATURATED FAT:** 0g; **CHOLESTEROL:** 0mg, **SODIUM:** 385mg; **TOTAL CARBOHYDRATE:** 42g; **FIBER:** 11g; **PROTEIN:** 9g

FAT-FREE REFRIED BEANS

 SERVES: 8

 PREP: 5 MINUTES
PRESSURE: 40 MINUTES
TOTAL: 1 HOUR

 SETTINGS: SAUTÉ (MEDIUM),
PRESSURE COOK (HIGH)
RELEASE: NATURAL

2 cups dried pinto beans

1 yellow onion, diced

4½ cups vegetable broth, divided

3 cloves garlic, minced

1 jalapeño, deseeded and diced

2 tsp ground cumin

½ tsp chili powder

1 tsp sea salt

Fresh cilantro, for garnish

These easy refried beans taste like they are from a Mexican restaurant and are delicious in tacos, burritos, and burrito bowls. Once you know this recipe, you'll never buy the cans again.

1 Pick out any debris or shriveled beans, then rinse and drain. Select **Sauté (Medium),** and heat the inner pot. Dry sauté the onion until softened and golden, 3 to 5 minutes. Press **Cancel.** Add ¼ cup broth to deglaze the pot, scraping up any pieces of onion that may be stuck to the bottom.

2 Add the garlic, jalapeño, remaining 4¼ cups broth, cumin, chili powder, and beans. Lock the lid and ensure the steam release valve is set to the sealing position. Select **Pressure Cook (High),** and set the cook time for **40 minutes.**

3 Once the cook time is complete, allow the pressure to release naturally. Season to taste with salt. Use a potato masher to mash the beans to the desired consistency. You can use Sauté (Medium) to reduce excess liquid, but keep in mind the beans will thicken significantly as they cool.

4 Garnish with cilantro and enjoy immediately with Mexican Rice (see p115) and veggies or tacos, or keep in an airtight container in the refrigerator for up to 3 days.

tip *Dried, unsoaked beans are great to use for mashed beans. They may break apart, but that's just fine in this recipe.*

Nutrition per serving:
CALORIES: 167; **TOTAL FAT:** 0g; **SATURATED FAT:** 0g; **CHOLESTEROL:** 0mg;
SODIUM: 602mg; **TOTAL CARBOHYDRATE:** 31g; **FIBER:** 11g; **PROTEIN:** 9g

MEXICAN RICE

Flavorful Mexican rice is easier than ever thanks to the Instant Pot. This version gets a mildly spicy kick from fire-roasted tomatoes and jalapeño and earthy notes from cumin.

 SERVES: 6

 PREP: 2 MINUTES
PRESSURE: 4 MINUTES
TOTAL: 20 MINUTES

 SETTINGS: SAUTÉ (MEDIUM), PRESSURE COOK (HIGH)
RELEASE: NATURAL, QUICK

1 Select **Sauté (Medium),** and heat the oil, if using, in the inner pot until hot. (Otherwise, you can dry sauté in the hot pot or add a bit of water in the bottom of the pot.) Add the onion and saute until softened and golden, 3 to 5 minutes. Add the garlic and jalapeño, if using, and sauté 1 minute more. Add the broth and deglaze the pot, scraping up any pieces of onion that may be stuck to the bottom.

2 Stir in the rice, salt, and cumin. Add the tomatoes on top, but do not stir in; keeping the tomatoes on top ensures the rice steams without burning on the bottom.

3 Lock the lid and ensure the steam release valve is set to the sealing position. Select **Pressure Cook (High),** and set the cook time for **4 minutes.**

4 Once the cook time is complete, allow the pressure to release naturally 5 minutes, then quick release any remaining pressure. Carefully remove the lid. Stir in the tomatoes and serve warm.

2 tbsp extra virgin olive oil (optional)

1 cup diced yellow onion

3 cloves garlic, minced

1 jalapeño (optional), deseeded and roughly chopped

2½ cups vegetable broth

2 cups white Basmati rice, rinsed and well drained

1 tsp sea salt

1 tbsp ground cumin

1 (15oz; 420g) can fire-roasted diced tomatoes, undrained

tip *This Mexican rice is delicious wrapped up in tortillas with Fat-Free Refried Beans (see p114).*

Nutrition per serving:
CALORIES: 323; **TOTAL FAT:** 6g; **SATURATED FAT:** 1g; **CHOLESTEROL:** 0mg; **SODIUM:** 742mg; **TOTAL CARBOHYDRATE:** 63g; **FIBER:** 2g; **PROTEIN:** 6g

SALADS & SIDES   115

SERVES: 4

 PREP: 1 MINUTE
PRESSURE: 4 MINUTES
TOTAL: 25 MINUTES

 SETTINGS: PRESSURE COOK (HIGH)
RELEASE: NATURAL

1 cup basmati rice, rinsed
and drained

1 cup water

¼ tsp sea salt

BASIC WHITE BASMATI RICE

Basmati rice makes an excellent quick-and-easy base for stews and curries. This recipe can be used for other types of long-grain white rice, such as jasmine.

1 Add all ingredients to the inner pot. Lock the lid and ensure the steam release valve is set to the sealing position. Select **Pressure Cook (High),** and set the cook time for **4 minutes.**

2 Once the cook time is complete, allow the pressure to release naturally. Carefully remove the lid, stir, and transfer the rice to a serving bowl. Serve immediately.

Nutrition per serving:
CALORIES: 169; **TOTAL FAT:** 0g; **SATURATED FAT:** 0g; **CHOLESTEROL:** 0mg; **SODIUM:** 150mg; **TOTAL CARBOHYDRATE:** 37g; **FIBER:** 0.5g; **PROTEIN:** 3g

 SERVES: 4

 PREP: 1 MINUTE
PRESSURE: 22 MINUTES
TOTAL: 43 MINUTES

 SETTINGS: PRESSURE COOK (HIGH)
RELEASE: NATURAL

1 cup long-grain brown rice,
rinsed and drained

1 cup water

¼ tsp sea salt

BASIC LONG-GRAIN BROWN RICE

Brown rice has a nuttier flavor and chewier texture than white. While it does take longer to cook than white rice, the Instant Pot cuts the standard cooking time in half.

1 Add all ingredients to the inner pot. Lock the lid and ensure the steam release valve is set to the sealing position. Select **Pressure Cook (High),** and set the cook time for **22 minutes.**

2 Once the cook time is complete, allow the pressure to release naturally. Carefully remove the lid, stir, and transfer the rice to a serving bowl. Serve immediately.

Nutrition per serving:
CALORIES: 172; **TOTAL FAT:** 1.5g; **SATURATED FAT:** 0g; **CHOLESTEROL:** 0mg; **SODIUM:** 149mg; **TOTAL CARBOHYDRATE:** 36g; **FIBER:** 2g; **PROTEIN:** 4g

PERFECT QUINOA

 SERVES: 6

The Instant Pot makes perfectly fluffy quinoa easier than ever. This is an easy recipe to memorize because it's all about the 1's: 1 cup quinoa, 1 cup water, 1 minute. Use your quinoa as a base for curries, salads, and veggie bowls, or dress it with a little olive oil and herbs for a side dish.

 PREP: 2 MINUTES
PRESSURE: 1 MINUTE
TOTAL: 30 MINUTES

 SETTINGS: PRESSURE COOK (HIGH)
RELEASE: NATURAL

1 cup quinoa
1 cup water
¼ tsp sea salt
1 tsp extra virgin olive oil (optional)

1   Rinse the quinoa in a fine-mesh sieve to remove any bitterness on the outer layer. Drain and add to the inner pot. Add 1 cup water and sea salt. Lock the lid and ensure the steam release valve is set to the sealing position. Select **Pressure Cook (High),** and set the cook time for **1 minute.**

2   Once the cook time is complete, allow the pressure to release naturally. Carefully remove the lid and fluff the quinoa with a spoon or fork. Drizzle with a little olive oil for flavor, if desired. Season to taste with more salt.

3   Transfer to a serving bowl and serve immediately. Once the lid has been removed, don't let the quinoa sit in the warm pot for longer than 10 minutes or it will start to dry out.

tip *You can add more flavor to this basic quinoa by stirring in garlic salt, fresh chopped herbs, or a squeeze of lemon or lime juice. Cilantro and lime are great for Mexican-inspired burrito bowls.*

Nutrition per ½ cup (excluding olive oil):
CALORIES: 104; **TOTAL FAT:** 1.5g; **SATURATED FAT:** 0g; **CHOLESTEROL:** 0mg; **SODIUM:** 98mg; **TOTAL CARBOHYDRATE:** 18g; **FIBER:** 2g; **PROTEIN:** 4g

SNACKS & APPETIZERS

SERVES: 2

 PREP: 5 MINUTES, PLUS OVERNIGHT
FOR SOAKING
PRESSURE: 15 MINUTES
TOTAL: 30 MINUTES

 SETTINGS: STEAM (HIGH)
RELEASE: QUICK

1 cup water

1 large artichoke (about 4½ in;
11.5cm in diameter), or 3 medium
artichokes

Juice of ½ lemon

FOR THE AIOLI DIPPING SAUCE:

½ cup raw cashews, soaked
overnight or 2 hours in hot water

1½ tbsp Dijon mustard

1 tbsp apple cider vinegar

Juice of ½ lemon

2 cloves garlic

Pinch of ground turmeric

½ tsp sea salt

⅓ cup water

STEAMED ARTICHOKE
with Vegan Dijon Aioli

Creamy, zippy, and garlicky mustard aioli dipping sauce adds
flavor to steamed artichokes. Don't forget to eat the best part—
the artichoke hearts!

1 Fit the inner pot with the trivet or steam rack, and add 1 cup water.
Trim the artichoke stem so that it is 1 to 2 inches (2.5–5cm) long, and
trim about 1 inch (2.5cm) off the top. Squeeze the lemon juice over the
top of the artichoke and add the lemon rind to the water. (This will add
flavor and help preserve the artichoke's color.) Place the artichoke,
top-side down, on the trivet.

2 Lock the lid and ensure the steam release valve is set to the sealing
position. Select **Steam (High),** and set the cook time for **15 minutes
for one large artichoke,** or **10 minutes for 3 medium artichokes.**

3 Once the cook time is complete, immediately quick release the
pressure. Carefully remove the lid and check for doneness—leaves
should be easy to remove and the "meat" at the base of each leaf
should be tender. If the artichoke is not yet done, place back on
the trivet and use **Pressure Cook (High),** cooking for 2 to 3 minutes
more until tender. You might need to add more water to account
for evaporation if adding more time.

4 Meanwhile, make the aioli dipping sauce. Drain the cashews and
place them in a blender. Add the Dijon, vinegar, lemon juice, garlic,
turmeric, and sea salt. Add half the water and blend. Continue adding
water as you blend until the sauce is smooth and creamy. Transfer the
sauce to a small bowl or jar. Refrigerate until ready to use.

5 Use tongs to remove the hot artichoke and place on a serving dish.
Serve the artichoke warm with the aioli.

tip *Whole artichokes can take anywhere from 6 to 12 minutes to cook
at high pressure and up to 17 minutes on steam mode, depending on the
size and age. Using the Steam setting retains the most vitamins and
minerals, as well as color. If you don't like very soft artichokes, it's best
to start with a lower time and add more minutes as needed.*

Nutrition per serving:
CALORIES: 78; **TOTAL FAT:** 4g; **SATURATED FAT:** 0.5g; **CHOLESTEROL:** 0mg;
SODIUM: 201mg; **TOTAL CARBOHYDRATE:** 9g; **FIBER:** 3g; **PROTEIN:** 3g

MAKES: 16 ROUNDS

PREP: 3 MINUTES
PRESSURE: 10 MINUTES, PLUS 3 MINUTES
TOTAL: 25 MINUTES

SETTINGS: PRESSURE COOK (LOW), SAUTÉ (MEDIUM)
RELEASE: QUICK

---

1 (18oz; 510g) package precooked polenta

Cooking spray, for coating

1oz (25g) dried porcini or dried mixed mushrooms (about 1 cup dry)

Water, to cover

8oz (225g) fresh cremini mushrooms, halved

4 cloves garlic, minced

4 sprigs fresh thyme

⅛ tsp sea salt

Freshly ground black pepper

Truffle salt (optional), for finishing

¼ cup freshly chopped flat-leaf parsley or basil

MUSHROOM POLENTA ROUNDS

These addictive small bites are party-ready and bursting with deep-flavored umami.

1 Preheat the oven to 425°F (220°C). Coat a baking sheet with cooking spray. Cut the polenta crosswise into ½-inch (1.25cm) rounds and place on the baking sheet. Coat the rounds with cooking spray. Bake for 15 minutes, flipping halfway.

2 Meanwhile, to rehydrate the dried mushrooms, add them to the inner pot and cover with 1 inch (2.5cm) of water. Lock the lid and ensure the steam release valve is set to the sealing position. Select **Pressure Cook (Low),** and set the cook time for **10 minutes.**

3 Once the cook time is complete, immediately quick release the pressure. Drain the rehydrated mushrooms through a fine-mesh sieve over a bowl to reserve the cooking liquid—this is an excellent mushroom broth to use later. Roughly chop the mushrooms.

4 Add the cremini mushroom halves and rehydrated mushrooms back into the pot. Add ½ cup mushroom broth. Top with the garlic, thyme, salt, and pepper.

5 Lock the lid and ensure the steam release valve is set to the sealing position. Select **Pressure Cook (High),** and set the cook time for **3 minutes.** Once the cook time is complete, immediately quick release the pressure.

6 Select **Sauté (Medium),** and reduce the liquid for 2 minutes. Remove the thyme stems.

7 Place the polenta rounds on a serving dish and spoon the mushroom mixture on top. Sprinkle with truffle salt, if using. Garnish with fresh parsley or basil. Enjoy warm.

tip *Dried mushrooms have deeper flavor and create a beautiful broth to use later in soups, stews, or risotto. Find them and truffle salt on Amazon or at Cost Plus World Market.*

Nutrition per round:
CALORIES: 33; **TOTAL FAT:** 0g; **SATURATED FAT:** 0g; **CHOLESTEROL:** 0mg; **SODIUM:** 109mg; **TOTAL CARBOHYDRATE:** 7g; **FIBER:** 1g; **PROTEIN:** 1g

ROASTED GARLIC CROSTINI

While this garlic isn't truly roasted, steaming and then broiling creates a similar result in much less time. Squeeze out the mild, soft, creamy garlic cloves and spread them on crostini to enjoy plain, or add some of your favorite toppings.

1 Fit the inner pot with the trivet or steam rack and add 1 cup water. Cut about ¼ inch (0.5cm) off the top of the garlic heads. Drizzle with 1 teaspoon oil and sprinkle with a pinch of salt. Place the garlic cut-side up onto the trivet.

2 Lock the lid and ensure the steam release valve is set to the sealing position. Select **Pressure Cook (High),** and set the cook time for **5 minutes.**

3 Once the cook time is complete, allow the pressure to release naturally. Carefully remove the lid.

4 Preheat the broiler. Use tongs to transfer the steamed garlic bulbs to a baking sheet. Place the bread slices on the baking sheet, as well. Drizzle the garlic with the remaining 1 teaspoon oil.

5 Transfer the sheet to the oven and broil until the tops of the garlic have browned and the bread is toasted, watching closely to ensure it doesn't burn. The toast may be done before the garlic.

6 Serve the "roasted" garlic bulbs on a platter with the toast and any additional toppings. To make the crostini, remove the garlic from the skin and spread 1 to 2 cloves of the soft garlic on the crostini. Sprinkle with a pinch of salt and top with any additional toppings. Enjoy warm or at room temperature.

 SERVES: 6

 PREP: 2 MINUTES
PRESSURE: 5 MINUTES
TOTAL: 30 MINUTES

 SETTINGS: PRESSURE COOK (HIGH)
RELEASE: NATURAL

---

1 cup water

2 heads garlic

2 tsp extra virgin olive oil, divided

Sea salt, to taste

1 small loaf crusty bread, such as ciabatta, cut into 6 slices

OPTIONAL TOPPINGS:

Baby arugula

Fresh basil

Roasted red peppers

Sun dried tomatoes

Halved cherry tomatoes

Grilled asparagus, eggplant, or zucchini

tip *This roasted garlic is also great added to mashed potatoes (see p109).*

This roasted garlic is also great added to mashed potatoes (see p109).

Nutrition per serving (excluding optional toppings):
CALORIES: 105; **TOTAL FAT:** 2g; **SATURATED FAT:** 0g; **CHOLESTEROL:** 0mg; **SODIUM:** 228mg; **TOTAL CARBOHYDRATE:** 18g; **FIBER:** 1g; **PROTEIN:** 3g

WHITE BEAN BRUSCHETTA

My family and I discovered bruschetta di fagioli in Tuscany, and it's been a favorite appetizer ever since. While not traditional, we like to add a slice of tomato under the beans. Crunchy, garlicky toasted bread topped with creamy white beans, olive oil, and parsley is a satisfying starter.

 SERVES: 10

 PREP: 10 MINUTES, PLUS OVERNIGHT FOR SOAKING
PRESSURE: 6 MINUTES
TOTAL: 36 MINUTES

SETTINGS: PRESSURE COOK (HIGH)
RELEASE: NATURAL

1 Add the beans, 4 cups water, minced garlic, rosemary, and sage to the inner pot. Lock the lid and ensure the steam release valve is set to the sealing position. Select **Pressure Cook (High),** and set the cook time for **6 minutes.**

2 Once the cook time is complete, allow the pressure to release naturally for 15 to 20 minutes. Carefully remove the lid and gently drain the beans in a colander. Transfer the beans to a bowl. Remove the rosemary stems. Dress with olive oil, salt, and pepper to taste.

3 Toast the bread slices in the oven, on a grill, or in a grill pan. Rub the warm toast on one side with the raw garlic halves to impart garlic flavor.

4 Top the toasted slices with tomato, then the beans. Top with a generous drizzle of olive oil, salt, and pepper. Garnish with chopped parsley. Enjoy warm or at room temperature.

1 cup dry cannellini beans, soaked overnight

4 cups water

4 cloves garlic, minced

2 sprigs rosemary

4 sage leaves

3 tbsp extra virgin olive oil, plus more to serve

Truffle salt (or sea salt), to taste

Freshly ground black pepper, to taste

1 loaf crusty bread, such as baguette or ciabatta, sliced

2 cloves garlic, peeled and halved

2 Roma tomatoes, sliced

¼ cup chopped flat-leaf parsley

tip *Using soaked beans and the natural pressure release helps prevent the beans from breaking apart. It's also best to use the minimal cook time for this recipe to avoid overly mushy beans, but the exact cook time may vary depending on size and age of beans.*

Nutrition per serving:
CALORIES: 188; **TOTAL FAT:** 5g; **SATURATED FAT:** 1g; **CHOLESTEROL:** 0mg; **SODIUM:** 238mg; **TOTAL CARBOHYDRATE:** 30g; **FIBER:** 4g; **PROTEIN:** 7g

MAKES: 1½ cups

PREP: 5 MINUTES, PLUS OVERNIGHT FOR SOAKING
PRESSURE: 2 MINUTES
TOTAL: 15 MINUTES

SETTINGS: PRESSURE COOK (HIGH)
RELEASE: QUICK

1⅓ cup water, divided

½ cup (1-in; 2.5cm cubes) peeled Yukon Gold potatoes

½ cup (1-in; 2.5 slices) peeled carrots

½ cup raw cashews, soaked overnight or at least one hour in hot water

1 tbsp garlic powder

1–2 jalapeños, deseeded

1 tsp tomato paste

1 tsp sea salt

¼ cup nutritional yeast

Hot sauce, to taste

FOR SERVING:

Homemade or store-bought salsa

Fresh cilantro, for garnish

1 bag tortilla chips (omit for oil-free)

2 carrots, peeled and cut into sticks

2 stalks celery, cut into sticks

1 red bell pepper, deseeded and cut into slices

CASHEW "QUESO" DIP

Creamy with a little kick of spicy, this queso dip uses cashews to imitate a cheesy dip. This is fun to serve on a Mexican-inspired party platter with guacamole, veggies, and chips.

1   Fit the inner pot with a steamer basket, and add 1 cup water. Place the potatoes and carrots in the steamer basket. Lock the lid and ensure the steam release valve is set to the sealing position. Select **Pressure Cook (High),** and set the cook time for **2 minutes.**

2   Once the cook time is complete, immediately quick release the pressure and carefully remove the lid. Check that the vegetables are tender. If they're not yet tender, lock the lid and pressure cook for 1 minute more.

3   Transfer the steamed veggies to a blender. Drain the cashews and add to the blender. Add the garlic powder, 1 jalapeño, tomato paste, salt, nutritional yeast, and remaining ⅓ cup water. Blend until completely smooth. Taste and add another jalapeño or hot sauce for heat. Blend in more water as needed to thin.

4   Use a rubber spatula to scoop the mixture into a small serving bowl. Top with ¼ cup salsa and a few cilantro leaves. Serve the queso dip warm on a platter with chips, carrots, celery, bell pepper, and a bowl of the remaining salsa.

tip *Cashew "Queso" Dip reheats beautifully. Store leftovers in an airtight container in the refrigerator for up to 3 days, or make ahead and reheat in the microwave for 1 minute. This is also great served with the guacamole on page 38.*

Nutrition per ¼ cup (excluding foods for serving):
CALORIES: 90; **TOTAL FAT:** 5g; **SATURATED FAT:** 0g; **CHOLESTEROL:** 0mg; **SODIUM:** 205mg; **TOTAL CARBOHYDRATE:** 9g; **FIBER:** 2g; **PROTEIN:** 4g

SICILIAN EGGPLANT CAPONATA

One of the most popular Sicilian appetizers, caponata is bursting with flavor from briny olives and capers, sweet tomatoes, and soft eggplant. This version is much easier and lower in oil than the traditional recipe, which calls for frying the eggplant in copious amounts of oil.

 SERVES: 8

 PREP: 10 MINUTES
PRESSURE: 3 MINUTES
TOTAL: 20 MINUTES

 SETTINGS: SAUTÉ (MEDIUM), PRESSURE COOK (LOW)
RELEASE: QUICK

1 Select **Sauté (Medium),** and heat the oil, if using, in the inner pot until hot. (Otherwise, you can dry sauté in the hot pot or add a bit of water in the bottom of the pot.) Add the onion and sauté until softened and golden, 3 to 5 minutes. Add half of the garlic and sauté 1 minute more. Add ⅓ cup water to deglaze the pan, scraping up any bits stuck to the bottom of the pot.

2 Layer the eggplant, celery, salt, pepper, and tomatoes, in that order, and do not stir. Lock the lid and ensure the steam release valve is set to the sealing position. Select **Pressure Cook (Low),** and set the cook time for **3 minutes.**

3 Once the cook time is complete, immediately quick release the pressure. Carefully remove the lid and make sure eggplant is tender. If not, lock the lid and pressure cook for 1 minute more.

4 Use a ladle to drain as much liquid as possible from the pot and discard. (You should be able to remove ½ to 1 cup of liquid.) Select **Sauté (Medium),** and simmer to cook off even more liquid for about 1 minute while stirring in the tomato paste. Stir in the remaining garlic, olives, capers, vinegar, and sugar.

5 Transfer the caponata to a glass storage container or serving bowl and garnish with parsley. Enjoy warm or cold on top of pasta or scooped up with sliced and toasted baguette.

2 tbsp extra virgin olive oil (optional)

1 small yellow onion, diced

2 cloves garlic, minced, divided

⅓ cup water

1 large eggplant (about 1lb; 450g), cut into 1-in (2.5cm) cubes

2 stalks celery, diced

½ tsp sea salt

¼ tsp red pepper flakes

4 Roma tomatoes, deseeded and chopped

2 tbsp tomato paste

⅓ cup pitted green olives, quartered

3 tbsp capers, drained

1 tbsp red wine vinegar

½ tbsp organic sugar

¼ cup chopped flat-leaf parsley

tip *There are many variations of caponata throughout Italy and the world. Some include raisins and toasted pine nuts—feel free to add them to the top of this recipe if you'd like.*

Nutrition per ½ cup:
CALORIES: 116; **TOTAL FAT:** 8g; **SATURATED FAT:** 0.5g; **CHOLESTEROL:** 0mg; **SODIUM:** 745mg; **TOTAL CARBOHYDRATE:** 9g; **FIBER:** 3.5g; **PROTEIN:** 2g

MAKES: ABOUT 15

PREP: 15 MINUTES
PRESSURE: 3 MINUTES
TOTAL: 45 MINUTES

SETTINGS: SAUTÉ (MEDIUM),
STEAM (HIGH)
RELEASE: QUICK

2 tbsp sesame or coconut oil, divided

½ small yellow onion, finely diced

1½ cups finely diced mushrooms

1 cup shredded carrots

2 cups shredded cabbage

2 tbsp freshly minced ginger

2 cloves garlic, minced

¼ cup chopped chives

2 tbsp soy sauce

1 package gyoza dumpling wrappers

1 cup water

1 tsp toasted sesame seeds

FOR THE DIPPING SAUCE:

⅓ cup soy sauce

2 tbsp rice vinegar

1 tbsp chives

tip *You can find gyoza wrappers at Asian grocery stores and some regular grocery stores, often next to the tofu. If you're avoiding oil, you can skip the step of frying them, but they won't have the classic crispy exterior.*

VEGGIE-PACKED POTSTICKERS

Flavorful dumplings packed with vegetables are steamed and then crisped up. These make a delicious appetizer or snack.

1 To make the filling, select **Sauté (Medium),** and heat 1 tablespoon oil in the inner pot. Add the onion and mushrooms and sauté until the onion is softened and golden, 3 to 5 minutes. Add the carrots, cabbage, ginger, garlic, and chives, and sauté until all the vegetables are tender and most of the liquid has evaporated, about 5 minutes. Add the soy sauce and simmer for 1 to 2 minutes more to reduce the liquid.

2 To make each potsticker, place a tablespoon-sized mound of the filling onto the center of a gyoza wrapper. Moisten the edges of the wrapper with water. Bring both sides up and pinch together over the center of the filling. Pinch all along the edge, creating pleats to seal. Set aside and continue until all of the filling has been used up.

3 If you used the inner pot to sauté, rinse and dry it, and place it back into the Instant Pot. Fit with the trivet or steam rack and fill with 1 cup water. Place a sheet of parchment paper, roughly the same size as the pot, over the rack to hold the potstickers. Place the potstickers on the parchment. If more room is needed, place a second piece of parchment on top, then add another layer of potstickers.

4 Lock the lid and ensure the steam release valve is set to the sealing position. Select **Steam (High),** and set the cook time for **3 minutes.** Once the cook time is complete, immediately quick release the pressure. Carefully remove the lid and the potstickers.

5 Select **Sauté (Medium),** and heat the remaining 1 tablespoon oil in the inner pot until hot, or use a skillet on the stovetop over medium-high heat. (Using the skillet is easiest, but both methods work.) Brown the potstickers on one or all sides. Transfer to a serving dish and immediately sprinkle with sesame seeds.

6 Meanwhile, make the dipping sauce. In a small bowl, whisk together all ingredients. Serve the potstickers warm with the dipping sauce.

Nutrition per potsticker (including dipping sauce):
CALORIES: 76; **TOTAL FAT:** 2g; **SATURATED FAT:** 0g; **CHOLESTEROL:** 0mg; **SODIUM:** 386mg; **TOTAL CARBOHYDRATE:** 14g; **FIBER:** 1.5g; **PROTEIN:** 3g

RED PEPPER HUMMUS

MAKES: ABOUT 2½ CUPS

PREP: 5 MINUTES
PRESSURE: 40 MINUTES
TOTAL: 1 HOUR 20 MINUTES

SETTINGS: PRESSURE COOK (HIGH)
RELEASE: NATURAL

1 cup dried chickpeas, rinsed

4 cups water

1 (12oz; 340g) jar roasted red bell peppers, drained and patted dry

¼ cup tahini

3 cloves garlic, roughly chopped

½ tsp sea salt

½ tsp smoked paprika

Pita bread, cut into triangles, for serving

Persian cucumbers, sliced, for serving

The Instant Pot makes last-minute homemade hummus a breeze since no soaking is required. This oil-free roasted red pepper version has extra flavor from fresh garlic and smoky peppers. Use as a dip for veggies and pita bread or as a spread for sandwiches and wraps.

1 Add the chickpeas and 4 cups water to the inner pot. Lock the lid and ensure the steam release valve is set to the sealing position. Select **Pressure Cook (High),** and set the cook time for **40 minutes.**

2 Once the cook time is complete, allow the pressure to release naturally. Carefully remove the lid and drain the chickpeas over a bowl to reserve the cooking liquid. Transfer the drained chickpeas to the bowl of a food processor. (Blending while the chickpeas are still warm results in a creamier hummus.) Reserve a 1-inch (2.5cm) piece of a red pepper for garnish, and add the rest of the red peppers to the food processor. Add the tahini, garlic, salt, and paprika.

3 Lock the lid of the food processor and blend until combined. Add the reserved cooking liquid, also known as *aquafaba*, 1 tablespoon at a time through the tube to help blend. Continue blending and adding aquafaba as needed until very smooth and creamy. You may need up to ¾ cup aquafaba.

4 Remove the lid and adjust the salt and paprika to taste. Transfer the hummus to a lidded container or serving bowl. Chop the remaining piece of roasted pepper and place on top for garnish. Refrigerate for at least 2 hours.

5 Once chilled, serve the hummus with pita bread and cucumbers, or use as a sandwich spread. Store leftovers in an airtight container in the refrigerator for up to 5 days.

tip *If you prefer to soak your chickpeas first, you can cut the pressure cook time down to 25 minutes.*

Nutrition per 2 tablespoons (excluding pita and cucumbers):
CALORIES: 55; **TOTAL FAT:** 2g; **SATURATED FAT:** 0g **CHOLESTEROL:** 0mg;
SODIUM: 55mg; **TOTAL CARBOHYDRATE:** 6g; **FIBER:** 2g; **PROTEIN:** 2g

SPINACH ARTICHOKE DIP

This easy, hot spinach artichoke dip is so creamy and delicious that no one would guess it's dairy-free. It's a crowd-pleasing party appetizer served with crackers and veggies.

 SERVES: 6

 PREP: 10 MINUTES, PLUS OVERNIGHT FOR SOAKING
PRESSURE: 20 MINUTES
TOTAL: 40 MINUTES

 SETTINGS: PRESSURE COOK (HIGH)
RELEASE: QUICK

1 Drain the soaked cashews and transfer to a blender. Add ½ cup water, nutritional yeast, garlic powder, salt, and pepper. Blend until very smooth and creamy, about 2 minutes. Add up to another ¼ cup water if needed to blend.

2 Cut the artichoke hearts into quarters and place in a medium bowl. Squeeze as much liquid as possible out of the thawed spinach. You can press it against a fine-mesh sieve or squeeze in a piece of cheesecloth or paper towel. Place the drained spinach into the bowl with the artichoke hearts.

3 Pour the cashew cream over the artichokes and spinach, and stir to combine. Transfer the mixture to an oven-safe baking dish, such as a 5 to 6-inch (12.5–15.25cm) soufflé dish. Cover the dish with foil.

4 Fit the inner pot with the trivet or steam rack, and add the remaining 1 cup water. Place the dish on the trivet. Lock the lid and ensure the steam release valve is in the sealing position. Select **Pressure Cook (High),** and set the cook time for **20 minutes.**

5 Once the cook time is complete, immediately quick release the pressure. Carefully remove the lid. Using potholders, remove the baking dish and foil. Garnish with green onion. Add a pinch more of sea salt and pepper to taste. Serve warm with the desired serving options.

1 cup raw cashews, soaked overnight or for 2 hours in hot water

1½ cups water, divided

⅛ cup nutritional yeast

1 tsp garlic powder

½ tsp sea salt

¼ tsp freshly ground black pepper

2 (14oz; 400g) cans artichoke hearts in water, drained and patted dry

1 (16oz; 450g) bag frozen chopped spinach, thawed

1 green onion, thinly sliced, for garnish

OPTIONS FOR SERVING:

Seed crackers

Sliced and toasted baguette

Carrot sticks

Sliced hothouse cucumber

tip *Nutritional yeast flavor can vary from brand to brand. I like Bragg's and Trader Joe's best.*

Nutrition per serving (excluding options for serving):
CALORIES: 230; **TOTAL FAT:** 12g; **SATURATED FAT:** 2g; **CHOLESTEROL:** 0mg; **SODIUM:** 335mg; **TOTAL CARBOHYDRATE:** 27g; **FIBER:** 15g; **PROTEIN:** 11g

VEGGIE SUSHI

Homemade sushi is so much fun, and it's easier to prepare than you might expect. These veggie rolls are filled with fresh, raw vegetables, such as creamy avocado and crunchy peppers.

 MAKES: 4 ROLLS; 32 (1-IN.; 2.5CM) PIECES

 PREP: 20 MINUTES
PRESSURE: 3 MINUTES
TOTAL: 1 HOUR

 SETTINGS: PRESSURE COOK (HIGH)
RELEASE: NATURAL

1   Rinse the rice in several changes of water until the water is clear. Drain and add the rice to the inner pot along with 2 cups water.

2   Lock the lid and ensure the steam release valve is set to the sealing position. Select **Pressure Cook (High),** and set the cook time for **3 minutes.**

3   Once the cook time is complete, allow the pressure to release naturally. Carefully remove the lid and stir the rice. Transfer to a bowl to cool.

4   To make each sushi roll, lay one piece of nori on a bamboo sushi mat or on a piece of parchment paper slightly larger than the nori sheet. Cover the nori with a thin layer of rice (about 1 cup), leaving 1 inch (2.5cm) bare at the top and bottom. Place a line of veggies along the edge closest to you. Sprinkle with a pinch of salt, if desired. Wrap that edge of nori over the veggies and continue to roll as tightly as possible until you form a log—use the bamboo mat or parchment to help to roll the sushi tightly. Seal the roll by brushing a little water where the edge meets the other side of the roll.

5   Use a very sharp chef's knife to cut the roll crosswise into 8 (1-in; 2.5cm) pieces. Sprinkle with sesame seeds.

6   Serve the sushi rolls immediately, or refrigerate until ready to eat. Serve with soy sauce or coconut aminos for dipping. Wasabi and pickled ginger add even more flavor for serving, but are optional.

2 cups dried sushi rice (such as Lundberg Family Farms Organic California Sushi Rice)

2 cups water

4 sheets sushi nori

1 large avocado, sliced

1 red bell pepper, deseeded and cut into thin strips

2 Persian cucumbers, thinly sliced lengthwise

1 cup shredded carrot

Sea salt (optional), to taste

2 tbsp toasted sesame seeds

FOR SERVING:

Soy sauce (or coconut aminos for gluten-free and soy-free)

Prepared wasabi (optional)

Pickled ginger (optional)

tip *You can find sushi rice in the rice section of many grocery stores, while nori will be in the Asian section. You can find both of these, as well as wasabi and pickled ginger, in most Asian grocery stores.*

Nutrition per roll (8 pieces) (excluding options for serving):
CALORIES: 458; **TOTAL FAT:** 7g; **SATURATED FAT:** 1g; **CHOLESTEROL:** 0mg; **SODIUM:** 210mg; **TOTAL CARBOHYDRATE:** 87g; **FIBER:** 8g; **PROTEIN:** 9g

SERVES: 2½ CUPS

PREP: 5 MINUTES
COOK: 4 HOURS
TOTAL: 5 HOURS

SETTINGS: SLOW COOK (LOW)
RELEASE: NONE

1 tbsp melted coconut oil, plus more to grease

⅓ cup pure maple syrup

1 tbsp coconut sugar

1 tsp pure vanilla extract

1 tsp ground cinnamon

¼ tsp sea salt

Large pinch of nutmeg

⅛ tsp cayenne pepper

2½ cups raw nuts (any combination of almonds, walnuts, and cashews)

SPICED NUTS

Cinnamon-spiced nuts have that irresistible balance of sweet and salty with a little kick of cayenne.

1 In a medium bowl, whisk together all ingredients except the nuts. Add the nuts and stir well to coat.

2 Grease the bottom of the inner pot with coconut oil. Transfer the nut mixture to the pot and spread into an even layer. Select **Slow Cook (Low),** and set the cook time for 4 hours. Cover with a glass lid, if you have one, or the standard lid with the steam release valve set to the venting position. Stir halfway through.

3 Once the cook time is complete, stir and transfer the nuts to a cookie sheet lined with parchment paper to cool for 1 hour. The nuts will crisp up as they cool. Store in an airtight glass container at room temperature for up to 3 weeks.

tip *These nuts make a wonderful homemade holiday or host gift!*

Nutrition per ¼ cup:
CALORIES: 155; **TOTAL FAT:** 11g; **SATURATED FAT:** 2g; **CHOLESTEROL:** 0mg; **SODIUM:** 2mg; **TOTAL CARBOHYDRATE:** 11g; **FIBER:** 2g; **PROTEIN:** 4g

POPCORN
with Special Seasoning

There's no need for microwavable popcorn bags when you can make natural popcorn in the Instant Pot! Homemade popcorn is a tasty, salty, low-calorie, whole grain snack that's always satisfying.

1 Select **Sauté (High),** and add the coconut oil to melt. Once the inner pot has reached maximum heat, add the popping corn and stir to coat well with the coconut oil. Cover with a vented glass lid. If you don't have a vented glass lid that fits the pot, you can use the standard lid set on top—but not locked—with the steam release valve set to the venting position. (This recipe will take longer when using the standard lid and result in fewer popped kernels, so using a glass lid is highly recommended.)

2 Cook for about 4 minutes, without removing the lid, until the popping slows and most of the kernels have popped. Press **Cancel.**

3 Immediately, while the popcorn is still hot, add your desired seasonings to taste. Stir to coat. Enjoy the popcorn warm or at room temperature.

 MAKES: ABOUT 6 CUPS

 PREP: 1 MINUTE
COOK: 4 MINUTES
TOTAL: 12 MINUTES

 SETTINGS: SAUTÉ (HIGH)
RELEASE: NONE

1½ tbsp coconut oil
½ cup organic popping corn

OPTIONAL FOR SEASONING:
Nutritional yeast and sea salt
Truffle salt
Dried rosemary and sea salt
Ground cinnamon and pure maple syrup

tip *Find organic popping corn in bulk bins and store in glass jars for the best value and environmental sustainability.*

Nutrition per cup (excluding options for seasoning):
CALORIES: 83; **TOTAL FAT:** 4g; **SATURATED FAT:** 3g; **CHOLESTEROL:** 0mg; **SODIUM:** 0mg; **TOTAL CARBOHYDRATE:** 13g; **FIBER:** 3g; **PROTEIN:** 2g

DESSERTS

SERVES: 8

PREP: 15 MINUTES
PRESSURE: 50 MINUTES
TOTAL: 2 HOURS,
INCLUDING COOLING

SETTINGS: CAKE (HIGH) OR
PRESSURE COOK (HIGH)
RELEASE: NATURAL

1 cup water

1 cup gluten-free oat flour, or
gluten-free all-purpose flour

½ cup almond flour

1 tsp baking powder

1 tsp baking soda

2 tbsp arrowroot starch

¼ tsp sea salt

½ cup raw turbinado sugar

1 tsp ground cinnamon

¼ tsp nutmeg

¼ tsp ground ginger

1 cup grated carrots

½ cup chopped walnuts, plus
more for garnish

⅓ cup raisins

½ cup almond milk or other
plant-based milk

2 tbsp cashew butter

½ tsp pure vanilla extract

2 vegan eggs (see tip)

FOR THE FROSTING:

½ cup vegan cream cheese
(such as Kite Hill, Miyoko's, or
homemade)

1 tbsp pure maple syrup

Seeds from ½ vanilla bean, or
½ tbsp vanilla bean paste
(optional)

GLUTEN-FREE CARROT SNACK CAKE

This lightly sweet carrot, nut, and raisin cake has a tangy "cream cheese" topping. It is delightful for brunch, tea, or dessert.

1 Coat a 7-inch (17.5cm) springform pan with cooking spray or grease with coconut oil. Fit the inner pot with the trivet or steam rack, and fill with 1 cup water.

2 In a medium bowl, whisk together the oat flour, almond flour, baking powder, baking soda, arrowroot, salt, sugar, cinnamon, nutmeg, and ginger. Stir in the carrots, walnuts, and raisins.

3 In another medium bowl, whisk together the almond milk, cashew butter, vanilla, and vegan eggs.

4 Fold the wet ingredients into the dry ingredients until combined. Spread the batter into the prepared pan. Cover the pan with foil. Place the pan on the trivet.

5 Lock the lid and ensure the steam release valve is set to the sealing position. Select **Cake (High)**—if your pot has that function—or **Pressure Cook (High),** and set the cook time for **50 minutes.**

6 Once the cook time is complete, allow the pressure to release naturally for 5 minutes, then quick release any remaining pressure. Carefully remove the lid and lift the pan out of the pot. Discard the foil and set the pan on a cooling rack to cool completely before cutting. Remove the sides from the springform pan.

7 To make the frosting, in a small bowl, whisk together all ingredients. Add any additional maple syrup to taste. Spread the frosting onto the cooled cake and sprinkle with walnuts for garnish. Enjoy immediately. If not serving the whole cake at once, you may want to frost each piece individually just before eating because the cream cheese dries out quickly. Store covered in the refrigerator for up to 3 days.

tip *The best egg replacer I've found for baking is Bob's Red Mill Egg Replacer, but you can also use flax eggs. To make two flax eggs, whisk together 2 tablespoons flax meal and ¼ cup water. Let sit for 5 minutes until gelled.*

Nutrition per serving:
CALORIES: 257; **TOTAL FAT:** 13g; **SATURATED FAT:** 4g; **CHOLESTEROL:** 0mg;
SODIUM: 131mg; **TOTAL CARBOHYDRATE:** 32g; **FIBER:** 3g; **PROTEIN:** 6g

SERVES: 4

 PREP: 10 MINUTES
PRESSURE: 9 MINUTES
TOTAL: 30 MINUTES

 SETTINGS: PRESSURE COOK (HIGH)
RELEASE: QUICK

1 cup water

1pt (470ml) vegan vanilla ice cream (optional), for serving

FOR THE FILLING:

3½ cups peeled and diced Granny Smith apples (1-in; 2.5cm chunks) (about 3 large apples)

1 tbsp fresh lemon juice

1 tbsp fresh orange juice

½ tsp ground cinnamon

2 tsp coconut sugar

FOR THE TOPPING:

½ cup almond flour

½ cup old-fashioned rolled oats (certified gluten-free, if needed)

¼ cup coconut sugar

¼ tsp sea salt

3 tbsp vegan butter (such as Miyoko's or Earth Balance)

1 tbsp pure maple syrup

INDIVIDUAL APPLE CRISPS

Classic apple crisps made in ramekins with a nutty almond flour and oat-based topping are a beautiful and wholesome dessert.

1 To make the filling, in a medium bowl, toss together all ingredients. Portion the filling into 4 (8fl oz; 240ml) ramekins, filling all the way to the top. Cover the ramekins with foil.

2 Fit the inner pot with the trivet or steam rack, and add 1 cup water. Place the ramekins on the trivet. Lock the lid and ensure the steam release valve is set to the sealing position. Select **Pressure Cook (High),** and set the cook time for **9 minutes.** Once the cook time is complete, immediately quick release the pressure.

3 Meanwhile, prepare the topping. Place all the ingredients in the bowl of a food processor, and pulse a few times to combine. You can alternatively use your fingers to make the crumble. Preheat the oven to 500°F (260°C).

4 Carefully remove the lid and the ramekins. Remove the foil and make sure the apples are tender. If they're not, lock the lid and pressure cook for 1 minute more.

5 Spoon the desired amount of topping evenly over the apple mixture. (You may have leftovers.) Transfer the ramekins to the oven, and bake until the topping is golden brown, about 4 minutes. Enjoy warm with a scoop of ice cream on top, if desired.

tip *You can prepare the filling and the topping early in the day; store them in the refrigerator and cook when you're ready.*

Nutrition per serving (excluding ice cream):
CALORIES: 335; **TOTAL FAT:** 15g; **SATURATED FAT:** 3g; **CHOLESTEROL:** 0mg; **SODIUM:** 145mg; **TOTAL CARBOHYDRATE:** 35g; **FIBER:** 7g; **PROTEIN:** 5g

REFINED-SUGAR-FREE BLUEBERRY PIE

Fresh blueberry pie filling bakes inside the Instant Pot while the gluten-free almond flour crust crisps up in the oven. Serve this juicy pie with a scoop of vanilla ice cream and an extra crust "cookie."

 SERVES: 6

 PREP: 10 MINUTES
PRESSURE: 13 MINUTES
TOTAL: 45 MINUTES

 SETTINGS: PRESSURE COOK (HIGH)
RELEASE: QUICK

1 cup water
1pt (470ml) vegan vanilla ice cream, for serving
Fresh mint leaves, for serving

FOR THE FILLING:
4 cups fresh blueberries
1 tbsp fresh lemon juice
3 tbsp corn starch
3 tbsp coconut sugar

FOR THE CRUST:
2 cups blanched almond flour
¼ cup arrowroot starch
¼ tsp sea salt
4 tbsp melted coconut oil
2 tbsp pure maple syrup

1. To make the filling, in a medium bowl, toss together all ingredients. Transfer to a baking dish that will fit inside the inner pot, such as a glass Pyrex or soufflé dish. A 7 x 3-inch (17.5 x 7.5cm) soufflé dish is ideal. Cover with foil.

2. Fit the inner pot with the trivet or steam rack, and add 1 cup water. Place the dish on the trivet. Lock the lid and ensure the steam release valve is set to the sealing position. Select **Pressure Cook (High),** and set the cook time for **13 minutes.**

3. Once the cook time is complete, immediately quick release the pressure. Carefully remove the lid and the dish from the pot and discard the foil. Stir the filling if you'd like to break up the berries more. Let the filling cool for at least 15 minutes to thicken up.

4. Meanwhile, make the crust. In a medium bowl, whisk together the almond flour, arrowroot, and salt. Make a well in the middle and add the coconut oil and syrup. Stir into the dry ingredients until the dough comes together. On a piece of parchment or a silicone baking mat, roll the dough into a ¼-inch (0.5cm) thick circle slightly smaller than the dish containing the filling. Use a small, 1 to 3-inch (2.5–7.5cm) cookie cutter to cut a piece out of the center (optional) and cut more shapes from the remaining dough. Slide the parchment or silicone mat onto a cookie sheet. Transfer to the freezer for 10 minutes. Preheat the oven to 375°F (190°C).

5. Bake the pie crust circle and "cookies" until golden, about 10 minutes.

6. Let the pie crust cool. Carefully place the round piece atop the blueberry filling. Cut the pie into 8 servings, and serve in bowls with a scoop of ice cream and the small crust shapes. Garnish with fresh mint leaves.

tip *Feel free to use store-bought frozen vegan pie crust in a pinch, though the exact bake time may vary.*

Nutrition per serving:
CALORIES: 262; **TOTAL FAT:** 14g; **SATURATED FAT:** 8g; **CHOLESTEROL:** 0mg; **SODIUM:** 80mg; **TOTAL CARBOHYDRATE:** 35g; **FIBER:** 4g; **PROTEIN:** 3g

CHOCOLATE CAKE
with Dark Chocolate Ganache

Moist chocolate cake topped with silky dark chocolate ganache, fresh raspberries, and crunchy toasted hazelnuts is my all-time favorite dessert. No one would ever guess it's egg- and dairy-free.

SERVES: 10

PREP: 10 MINUTES
PRESSURE: 30 MINUTES
TOTAL: 1 HR 30 MINUTES

SETTINGS: CAKE (HIGH) OR PRESSURE COOK (HIGH)
RELEASE: NATURAL, QUICK

1 cup water

1 cup whole wheat pastry flour

½ cup unsweetened cocoa powder

½ cup raw turbinado sugar

1 tsp baking soda

½ tsp baking powder

½ tsp instant coffee

¼ tsp salt

¾ cup unsweetened almond milk

1 tbsp apple cider vinegar

1 tsp pure vanilla extract

¼ cup melted coconut oil

¼ cup chopped, toasted hazelnuts, for garnish

1 cup fresh raspberries, for garnish

Fresh mint leaves, for garnish

FOR THE GANACHE:

¾ cup chopped dairy-free dark chocolate

¼–⅓ cup canned coconut milk, stirred

1 Fill the inner pot with the trivet or steam rack, and add with 1 cup water. Coat a 7-inch (17.5cm) springform pan with cooking spray.

2 In a medium bowl, whisk together the flour, cocoa powder, sugar, baking soda, baking powder, instant coffee, and salt.

3 In another medium bowl, whisk together the almond milk, vinegar, vanilla, and oil. Stir the wet ingredients into the dry. Transfer the batter into the prepared pan and smooth into an even layer with the back of a spoon.

4 Cover the pan with foil and place on the trivet. Lock the lid and ensure the steam release valve is set to the sealing position. Select **Cake (High)**—if your pot has that function—or **Pressure Cook (High),** and set the cook time for **30 minutes.**

5 Once the cook time is complete, allow the pressure to release naturally for 10 minutes, then quick release any remaining pressure. Carefully remove the lid and the cake pan. Remove the foil and let the cake cool completely on a cooling rack.

6 Meanwhile, make the ganache. Place the chocolate in a small glass bowl. Heat the coconut milk in a small saucepan, or in the Instant Pot on **Sauté (Medium),** until it just begins to simmer. Carefully pour the coconut milk over the chocolate and stir until all the chocolate has melted and the mixture is smooth.

7 Pour the ganache over the top of the cooled cake, letting it drip down the sides. Garnish by arranging the berries, hazelnuts, and mint over the ganache. (I like to do this in a decorative crescent moon shape!)

8 Serve the cake at room temperature with more of the ganache, raspberries, and hazelnuts on the side, if desired.

tip *Substitute all-purpose or gluten-free 1:1 baking blend, if desired.*

Nutrition per serving:
CALORIES: 205; **TOTAL FAT:** 12g; **SATURATED FAT:** 8g; **CHOLESTEROL:** 0mg;
SODIUM: 204mg; **TOTAL CARBOHYDRATE:** 25g; **FIBER:** 3g; **PROTEIN:** 3g

DESSERTS

CHOCOLATE FONDUE

 MAKES: ABOUT 1½ CUPS

 PREP: 2 MINUTES
COOK: 5 MINUTES
TOTAL: 10 MINUTES

 SETTINGS: SLOW COOK (MEDIUM),
WARM (LOW)
RELEASE: NONE

9oz (255g) dairy-free chocolate
chips or chunks

1 cup canned full-fat coconut milk,
stirred, plus more as needed

1 tsp pure vanilla extract

Pinch of sea salt

FOR SERVING:

1pt (551ml) strawberries

½pt (276ml) raspberries

2 bananas, sliced

Rich chocolate fondue requires just a few ingredients and a few minutes for the most fun dessert around.

1 In the inner pot, stir together all ingredients. Select **Slow Cook (Medium),** and cover with a glass lid, or other lid that fits the pot. Stir occasionally until the chocolate has just melted, about 5 minutes. Select **Cancel** so that the chocolate doesn't burn. Add additional coconut milk to thin to the desired consistency.

2 Select **Warm (Low)**. Serve the fondue right from the Instant Pot to keep warm, or transfer to a small serving bowl. Serve with fruit and skewers for dipping.

tip You can use dark or semisweet chocolate for this recipe, depending on personal preference. There are several brands that make allergy-friendly chocolate, such as Enjoy Life.

Nutrition per 1 tablespoon (excluding foods for serving):
CALORIES: 67; **TOTAL FAT:** 5g; **SATURATED FAT:** 4g; **CHOLESTEROL:** 0mg; **SODIUM:** 9mg; **TOTAL CARBOHYDRATE:** 7g; **FIBER:** 1g; **PROTEIN:** 0g

GIANT CHOCOLATE CHUNK COOKIE

Made all in one bowl, these soft and rich almond flour cookies feature big, melty chunks of chocolate. This is the ultimate gluten-free and vegan treat.

 SERVES: 8

 PREP: 5 MINUTES
PRESSURE: 6 MINUTES
TOTAL: 40 MINUTES

 SETTINGS: PRESSURE COOK (HIGH)
RELEASE: NATURAL, QUICK

1 In a medium bowl, whisk together the almond flour, arrowroot, baking soda, and salt.

2 Make a well in the middle of the dry ingredients. Pour the coconut oil, maple syrup, and vanilla into the well, and whisk to combine the wet ingredients. Then whisk to combine with the dry ingredients. Stir in the dark chocolate. The mixture may be a little crumbly but should hold together when pressed.

3 Cut out a piece of parchment paper to fit the bottom of a 7-inch (17.5cm) springform pan. Press the dough firmly on top of the parchment. (Using the back of a measuring cup to press down can help create an even layer.) Cover the pan with foil.

4 Fit the inner pot with the trivet or steam rack, and add 1 cup water. Place the foil-covered springform pan onto the trivet. Lock the lid and ensure the steam release valve is set to the sealing position. Select **Pressure Cook (High),** and set the cook time for **6 minutes.**

5 Once the cook time is complete, allow the pressure to release naturally for 6 minutes, then quick release any remaining pressure. Preheat the oven broiler.

6 Carefully remove the lid and take the pan out of the inner pot. Remove the sides of the springform pan.

7 Transfer the cookie (still resting on the bottom of the springform pan) under the broiler for 1 minute, or just until golden on top. Let the cookie cool for 10 minutes, then cut into 8 wedges and serve.

2 cups super-fine blanched almond flour

3 tbsp arrowroot starch

1 tsp baking soda

¼ tsp sea salt

4 tbsp melted coconut oil

2 tbsp pure maple syrup

1 tsp pure vanilla extract

⅓ cup chopped dairy-free dark chocolate

1 cup water

tip *These cookies are quite rich, so feel free to cut them into even smaller portions. I find just a sliver is enough to satisfy.*

SERVES: 4

 PREP: 5 MINUTES
PRESSURE: 2 MINUTES
TOTAL: 12 MINUTES

 SETTINGS: PRESSURE COOK (LOW)
RELEASE: QUICK

2 medium-sized, just-ripe, firm peaches (white or yellow)

¼ cup almond flour

⅛ cup old-fashioned rolled oats (certified gluten-free, if needed)

⅛ cup chopped pecans

⅛ cup coconut sugar

Pinch of sea salt

1 tbsp vegan butter (such as Miyoko's or Earth Balance), melted

1 tbsp pure maple syrup

⅔ cup water

1pt (470ml) vegan vanilla ice cream (optional), for serving

Fresh mint (optional), for garnish

Ground cinnamon (optional), for garnish

CRUMBLY OAT STUFFED PEACHES

This beautiful summer dessert features juicy warm peaches, a crumbly oat and pecan topping, and vanilla ice cream.

1 Cut the peaches in half. Carefully remove the pits. If they don't easily come out, use a melon baller, taking care not to remove much of the peach flesh.

2 In a small bowl, stir together the almond flour, oats, pecans, coconut sugar, and salt. Pour in the melted butter and syrup, and stir to combine into a crumbly topping. Top the cut sides of the peaches evenly with the topping mixture.

3 Fit the inner pot with the trivet or steam rack, and add ⅔ cup water. Cover the trivet with a small piece of parchment paper. Place the peaches cut-side up on the parchment.

4 Lock the lid and ensure the steam release valve is set to the sealing position. Select **Pressure Cook (Low),** and set the cook time for **2 minutes.**

5 Once the cook time is complete, immediately quick release the pressure and carefully remove the lid. Check that the peaches are tender. If not, pressure cook for 1 minute more.

6 To crisp the topping, place the peaches onto a baking sheet and place under the broiler for 2 minutes, or until golden. (This step is optional but encouraged.)

7 Serve the stuffed peaches warm, topped with a scoop of ice cream, if desired, and garnished with fresh mint leaves and cinnamon, if using.

tip The trick to perfectly cooked Instant Pot stuffed peaches is to use peaches that are barely ripe and to leave as much flesh as possible around the pit. If not, your peaches may fall apart.

Nutrition per serving (excluding ice cream):
CALORIES: 150; **TOTAL FAT:** 8g; **SATURATED FAT:** 1g; **CHOLESTEROL:** 0mg; **SODIUM:** 24mg; **TOTAL CARBOHYDRATE:** 14g; **FIBER:** 2g; **PROTEIN:** 3g

SPICED POACHED PEARS

 SERVES: 4

 PREP: 10 MINUTES
PRESSURE: 5 MINUTES
TOTAL: 1 HOUR 15 MINUTES

 SETTINGS: PRESSURE COOK (HIGH), SAUTÉ (HIGH)
RELEASE: NATURAL

2 cups water

4 cups natural apple juice

½ lemon

1 tbsp freshly grated ginger

5 cardamom pods

2 cinnamon sticks

1 vanilla bean, or 1 tbsp vanilla bean paste

4 ripe d'Anjou pears, peeled

Vegan vanilla ice cream or Chocolate Cake with Dark Chocolate Ganache (see p143), for serving

Warm, soft, spiced pears are an elegant dessert, and this version has none of the added sugar or wine with which they're traditionally made. Serve alone, with vanilla ice cream, or with chocolate cake.

1 To the inner pot, add 2 cups water, apple juice, juice from the lemon, ginger, cardamom, and cinnamon. Add the lemon half. Cut the vanilla bean in half lengthwise and scrape the seeds into the pot. Add the pears. If they are not covered with liquid, add more water or apple juice.

2 Lock the lid and ensure the steam release valve is set to the sealing position. Select **Pressure Cook (High),** and set the cook time for **5 minutes.**

3 Once the cook time is complete, allow the pressure to release naturally.

4 Use a slotted spoon to remove the pears. To reduce and concentrate the flavors in the liquid, select **Sauté (High),** and simmer for 20 minutes, if desired.

5 Serve the pears in bowls with ice cream or chocolate cake and pour more of the cooking liquid over.

tip *Poached pears can be made early in the day and reheated or eaten cold. Store them in their cooking liquid.*

Nutrition per serving (including ½ cup cooking liquid):
CALORIES: 161; **TOTAL FAT:** 0g; **SATURATED FAT:** 0g; **CHOLESTEROL:** 0mg; **SODIUM:** 6mg; **TOTAL CARBOHYDRATE:** 42g; **FIBER:** 6g; **PROTEIN:** 1g

SALTED DATE CARAMEL SAUCE

Instant Pot-softened dates transform into a creamy sauce that tastes remarkably like caramel, but without any added sugar.

MAKES: ABOUT 1 CUP

PREP: 1 MINUTE
PRESSURE: 1 MINUTE
TOTAL: 12 MINUTES

SETTINGS: PRESSURE COOK (HIGH)
RELEASE: QUICK

1 cup Medjool dates (about 10)

1 cup water

1 cup full-fat coconut milk

1 tsp pure vanilla extract

¼ tsp sea salt

OPTIONS FOR SERVING:

Granny Smith apple slices and chopped walnuts

Strawberries

Pretzels

Vegan vanilla ice cream

1   Add the dates and 1 cup water to the inner pot. Lock the lid and ensure the steam release valve is set to the sealing position. Select **Pressure Cook (High),** and set the cook time for **1 minute.**

2   Once the cook time is complete, immediately quick release the pressure. Carefully remove the lid. Use a slotted spoon to remove the dates and place on a cutting board. Carefully remove and discard the pits. (A knife and fork can make this easier when the dates are hot.)

3   Transfer the pitted dates to a blender or food processor. Add ½ cup coconut milk, vanilla, and salt. Blend, adding more coconut milk or water, as needed, to thin into a thick but pourable consistency. Continue blending until very smooth, scraping down the sides as needed—this will take several minutes.

4   Transfer the caramel to a small bowl or jar and serve immediately with the desired serving options, or store in an airtight container in the refrigerator for up to 5 days.

tip *You can heat up the caramel sauce in the microwave at 20-second intervals until warm and soft.*

Nutrition per 2 tablespoons (excluding options for serving):
CALORIES: 137; **TOTAL FAT:** 6g; **SATURATED FAT:** 5g; **CHOLESTEROL:** 0mg;
SODIUM: 43mg; **TOTAL CARBOHYDRATE:** 24g; **FIBER:** 2g; **PROTEIN:** 1g

DESSERTS   149

CHOCOLATE DESSERT HUMMUS

Dark chocolate hummus is sure to satisfy any chocolate craving, while providing a plant-based protein and fiber boost. It's the perfect dessert dip for fruit and cinnamon pita chips.

 MAKES: ABOUT 2 CUPS (16 SERVINGS)

 PREP: 5 MINUTES
PRESSURE: 40 MINUTES
TOTAL: 1 HOUR 10 MINUTES

 SETTINGS: PRESSURE COOK (HIGH)
RELEASE: NATURAL

½ cup dried chickpeas, rinsed

2 cups water

⅓ cup unsweetened cocoa powder

¼ cup cashew or almond butter

½ tsp pure vanilla extract

⅛ tsp sea salt

3 tbsp pure maple syrup

1 tbsp raw turbinado sugar

¼ cup canned coconut milk

Fresh mint, for garnish

OPTIONS FOR SERVING:
Strawberries
Sliced apples
Pretzels
Cinnamon pita chips

1 To cook the chickpeas, add the chickpeas and 2 cups water to the inner pot. Lock the lid and ensure the steam release valve is set to the sealing position. Select **Pressure Cook (High),** and set the cook time for **40 minutes.**

2 Once the cook time is complete, allow the pressure to release naturally. Carefully remove the lid. Drain and rinse the chickpeas, and transfer to the bowl of a food processor. Add the cocoa powder, cashew butter, vanilla, salt, maple syrup, sugar, and coconut milk.

3 Process until very smooth and creamy, occasionally stopping to scrape down the sides with a rubber spatula. It may take several minutes to achieve very smooth hummus. Add more coconut milk if needed to thin.

4 Transfer the hummus to a lidded food storage container or serving bowl. Serve with any combination of strawberries, apples, pretzels, and pita chips. Store in the refrigerator for up to 5 days.

tip *If you'd like to use pre-cooked chickpeas, you'll need 1½ cups for this recipe.*

Nutrition per 2 tablespoons (excluding options for serving):
CALORIES: 104; **TOTAL FAT:** 6g; **SATURATED FAT:** 3.5g; **CHOLESTEROL:** 0mg; **SODIUM:** 29mg; **TOTAL CARBOHYDRATE:** 12g; **FIBER:** 2g; **PROTEIN:** 3g

STAPLES

MAKES: ABOUT 10 CUPS, OR 2½ QT (2.5L)

 PREP: 5 MINUTES
PRESSURE: 30 MINUTES
TOTAL: 50 MINUTES

 SETTINGS: SAUTÉ (MEDIUM), SOUP (HIGH)
RELEASE: NATURAL, QUICK

1 tsp extra virgin olive oil (optional)

1 white onion, roughly chopped

1 whole head garlic (skin on), halved crosswise

2 carrots, roughly chopped

3 stalks celery, roughly chopped

2 tsp sea salt (optional)

Pinch of freshly ground black pepper

A few sprigs of fresh rosemary, parsley, or thyme

2 bay leaves

⅓ cup dried mushrooms, rinsed (or 2 dried shitakes) (see tip)

Water, to fill (about 3qt; 3l)

HOMEMADE VEGETABLE BROTH

Homemade broth is easy to make, and it's tastier and less expensive than store-bought broth. Use this simple broth in soups, risotto, and more.

1 Select **Sauté (Medium),** and heat the oil, if using, in the inner pot until hot. (Otherwise, you can dry sauté in the hot pot or add a bit of water in the bottom of the pot.) Add the onion, garlic, carrots, and celery. Sauté until the onion is softened and golden, 3 to 5 minutes. Add the salt (if using), herbs, and mushrooms. Add the water until it reaches about 1 inch (2.5cm) under the max-fill line. Select **Cancel.**

2 Lock the lid and ensure the steam release valve is set to the sealing position. Select **Soup (High)** or **Pressure Cook (High),** and set the cook time for **30 minutes.**

3 Once the cook time is complete, allow the pressure to release naturally for 10 minutes, then quick release any remaining pressure. Carefully remove the lid. Use a slotted spoon to remove the vegetables. Carefully pour the broth through a fine-mesh sieve into glass jars or another storage container. Season to taste with salt and pepper. Cool completely and store in the refrigerator for up to 3 days or in the freezer for several weeks.

tip *Mushrooms add richness and umami to an otherwise very light and fresh broth. Dried mushrooms, like used in the Mushroom Polenta Rounds (see p122) are best, but you can also use about 5 fresh cremini mushrooms sautéed with the other vegetables. A splash of soy sauce or a piece of kombu seaweed are other ways to add umami.*

Nutrition per 1 cup:
CALORIES: 15; **TOTAL FAT:** 0g; **SATURATED FAT:** 0g; **CHOLESTEROL:** 0mg; **SODIUM:** 140mg; **TOTAL CARBOHYDRATE:** 3g; **FIBER:** 0g; **PROTEIN:** 0g

ITALIAN SEASONING BLEND

This is the perfect salt-free blend for Italian soups, sauces, vegetables, and more.

1 Add the rosemary to a blender, and pulse to chop. Add the remaining spices and pulse again to combine.

2 Transfer to a small, lidded glass jar and store at room temperature for up to 6 months.

tip *When using this seasoning blend, keep in mind it is the herbs only and doesn't contain salt or pepper. Red pepper flakes, garlic (fresh or powdered), and salt are nice additions when using this to make your own Italian recipes.*

Nutrition per 1 teaspoon:
CALORIES: 4; **TOTAL FAT:** 0g; **SATURATED FAT:** 0g; **CHOLESTEROL:** 0mg; **SODIUM:** 0mg; **TOTAL CARBOHYDRATE:** 1g; **FIBER:** 0g; **PROTEIN:** 0g

 MAKES: ABOUT ½ CUP

 PREP: 1 MINUTE
PRESSURE: NONE
TOTAL: 3 MINUTES

 SETTINGS: NONE
RELEASE: NONE

2 tbsp dried whole rosemary
2 tbsp dried basil
2 tbsp dried oregano
2 tbsp dried parsley
1 tbsp ground thyme
1 tsp dried sage

ALMOND RICOTTA

 **MAKES:** ABOUT 2 CUPS

 PREP: 1 MINUTE, PLUS OVERNIGHT FOR SOAKING
PRESSURE: NONE
TOTAL: 6 MINUTES

 SETTINGS: NONE
RELEASE: NONE

2 cups raw, slivered almonds, soaked overnight (Trader Joe's recommended)
½ cup water
2 tbsp extra virgin olive oil
½ tsp truffle salt

This almond-based "ricotta cheese" tastes even better than the real thing! It's easy to make and can be used in your favorite Italian recipes or simply spread on crackers. The truffle salt is what gives this recipe its irresistible flavor—find it in Italian grocery stores or online.

1 Drain and rinse the soaked almonds. Transfer to a blender or food processor and add ½ cup water, olive oil, and the truffle salt.

2 Blend, slowly adding up to ½ cup more water as needed until the mixture resembles ricotta cheese in texture. This may take more blending than you first expect, at least 5 minutes. Continue scraping down the sides of the bowl with a rubber spatula until it's completely smooth and creamy without any bits of crunchy nuts.

3 Taste and add more salt and oil if desired. Transfer to an airtight container and keep in the refrigerator for up to 1 week or use immediately in your favorite recipes, such as Vegetable Lasagna (see p67).

Nutrition per ¼ cup:
CALORIES: 186; **TOTAL FAT:** 17g; **SATURATED FAT:** 0g; **CHOLESTEROL:** 0mg; **SODIUM:** 70mg; **TOTAL CARBOHYDRATE:** 6g; **FIBER:** 3g; **PROTEIN:** 6g

HOMEMADE BBQ SAUCE

 MAKES: ABOUT 1 CUP

 PREP: 2 MINUTES
COOK: 10 MINUTES
TOTAL: 12 MINUTES

 SETTINGS: NONE
RELEASE: NONE

1 cup tomato sauce

⅓ cup apple cider vinegar

1 tbsp pure maple syrup

2 tbsp vegan Worcestershire sauce (gluten-free, if needed) (see tip on p113)

1 tsp ground cumin

1 tsp garlic powder

¼ tsp smoked paprika

⅛ tsp cayenne pepper

½ tsp sea salt

Making your own barbecue sauce is easier than you think, and it cuts out a lot of the processed ingredients you'll find in store-bought varieties. This recipe has a balanced blend of flavors, and you have total control over how sweet and spicy you'd like to make it.

1 In a small saucepan, whisk all ingredients together. Simmer over low heat until thickened and reduced, about 10 minutes. Store in an airtight container in the refrigerator for up to 1 week.

Nutrition per 2 tablespoons:
CALORIES: 10; **TOTAL FAT:** 0g; **SATURATED FAT:** 0g; **CHOLESTEROL:** 0mg; **SODIUM:** 181mg; **TOTAL CARBOHYDRATE:** 2g; **FIBER:** 0g; **PROTEIN:** 0g

SIMPLE CASHEW CREAM

 MAKES: 1 CUP

 PREP: 1 HOUR OR OVERNIGHT TO SOAK
PRESSURE: NONE
TOTAL: 5 MINUTES

 SETTINGS: NONE
RELEASE: NONE

1 cup raw cashews, soaked overnight or in hot water for at least 1 hour

½ cup water

½ tsp sea salt

Once hydrated in water and blended, cashews transform into a decadent, silky smooth cream. It's perfect for adding richness to soups, drizzling over veggies, using as the base of a creamy salad dressing, and more. This is what makes the Creamy Broccoli Soup (see p84) creamy!

1 Drain the soaked cashews, then rinse and drain again. Place in the blender with ½ cup water and salt.

2 Blend until very smooth and creamy. Use immediately, or store in an airtight container in the refrigerator for up to 4 days.

tip *To avoid a nutty flavor, it's important to use raw cashews.*

Nutrition per ¼ cup:
CALORIES: 180; **TOTAL FAT:** 14g; **SATURATED FAT:** 0g; **CHOLESTEROL:** 0mg; **SODIUM:** 144mg; **TOTAL CARBOHYDRATE:** 10g; **FIBER:** 1g; **PROTEIN:** 6g

ALMOND MILK

Creamy homemade nut milks are easy to make, taste better, and are more economical than store-bought. Use this plain almond milk recipe in breakfast bowls, over Blueberry Baked Oatmeal (see p34), and more.

1 Place the almonds in a bowl or glass jar and cover with water. Cover the bowl and let soak overnight at room temperature.

2 Drain and rinse the soaked almonds and transfer to a high-speed blender. Add 2 to 3 cups filtered water and blend until smooth.

3 Pour the almond milk through a piece of cheesecloth into a large glass jar to strain the solids. Store tightly sealed in the refrigerator for up to 5 days.

MAKES: ABOUT 3 CUPS

PREP: 8 HOURS TO SOAK
PRESSURE: NONE
TOTAL: 5 MINUTES

SETTINGS: NONE
RELEASE: NONE

1 cup raw almonds
2–3 cups filtered water

tip *Making naturally sweetened vanilla almond milk is easy, too! Simply add a few pitted Medjool dates and ½ teaspoon pure vanilla extract before blending the almonds and water.*

Nutrition per ½ cup:
CALORIES: 31; **TOTAL FAT:** 2g; **SATURATED FAT:** 0g; **CHOLESTEROL:** 0mg; **SODIUM:** 0mg; **TOTAL CARBOHYDRATE:** 1g; **FIBER:** 0.5g; **PROTEIN:** 1g

INDEX

T–U–V

W–X–Y–Z

Publisher Mike Sanders
Editor Alexandra Elliott
Book Designer Rebecca Batchelor
Art Director William Thomas
Photographer Kelly Jordan Schuyler
Food Stylist Savannah Norris
Recipe Tester and Nutritional Analyst Dana Angelo White
Proofreaders Rick Kughen and Lisa Starnes
Indexer Celia McCoy

First American Edition, 2020
Published in the United States by DK Publishing
6081 E. 82nd Street, Indianapolis, Indiana 46250

Copyright © 2020 by Marina Delio
20 21 22 23 24   10 9 8 7 6 5 4 3 2
002-316437-JAN2020

ISBN 978-1-4654-9009-4
Library of Congress Catalog Number: 2019945965

Printed and bound in Canada

Photograph on page 6 © Kacie Jean Photography
All other images © Dorling Kindersley Limited
For further information see: www.dkimages.com

A WORLD OF IDEAS:
SEE ALL THERE IS TO KNOW

www.dk.com